HITLER, THE KAISER, AND ME:

An Academic's Procession

Produced for Robert G. L. Waite
by Storey Communications, Inc., Pownal, Vermont.

President: M. John Storey
Vice President: Martha M. Storey
Custom Publishing Director: Megan Kuntze
Custom Managing Editor: Janet Lape
Project Manager: Susan McKenna
Design and Production: Mary B. Minella

Library of Congress Catalog Card Number: 99-95596

Hitler, The Kaiser, And Me:

An Academic's Procession

———— by ————

Robert G. L. Waite

with Cartoons by Peter Waite

Williamstown, Massachusetts
18 February 1999

TABLE OF CONTENTS

Preface ... ix

Five Coffees and One Beer ... 1

Father Meets Mother and No Firewater ... 7

My Canadian Boyhood ... 10

Visiting the Dukhobors ... 13

My Father's Parodies and Puns ... 15

The Death of Granny Waite ... 19

My First Love Affair ... 21

Christmas in Franklin and the English Box ... 22

My Rescue at Rock Lake ... 24

Grandmother Carter, Encounter with a Mountie, and King Tut's Tomb ... 27

Winnipeg: Electricity, Flush Toilets, and Paved Roads ... 33

American School Days ... 38

Benson High School ... 42

High School Reunion and a Sixteen-Cent Tax ... 45

My Flirtation with Disaster ... 47

Macalester College and Sleeping with John Wilkes Booth ... 49

Kenneth Holmes and *Earning Our Heritage* ... 52

A Military Interlude:
The Night I Saved Our Country ... 55

Courtship and Marriage ... 59

Peanut Butter at Harvard Graduate School ... 62

History 1 and "One Dead Dawg" ... 68

Williamstown and Williams College ... 70

Aleksandr Fursenko at Williams ... 74

"Dutchy" Wahl and His Wife's Pitcher ... 77

"Don't Send Me Your Walking Wounded" and a *Flight into Egypt* ... 79

Shoeshine in New Orleans ... 81

Williams in China with First-Class Twiddlers ... 83

Deacon of the Church: *"I'll Be Seeing You"* ... 92

Interview with the Governor General of Canada ... 95

Germany and My Old Uncle Harry ... 99

The High Commissioner of Germany:
"I'd Rather Not Talk About It." ... 101

Ottobrunn bei München:
Hans and Käthe Thomamüller and Four Kinds of Kraut ... 103

The Thomamüllers in Williamstown ... 112

Linz, Leonding, and Vienna ... 115

Wald Trudering: "Sitting-Down Facilities" and an Erased Swastika ... 117

Lenin, Hitler, and the *Hofbräuhaus* ... 120

Ainmillerstrasse, Hitler's Seat, and "The Wild Chase" ... 122

Japanese Flip-Flops in Prague ... 125

In Search of Adolf Hitler ... 128

Vanguard of Nazism: The German Free Corps Movement ... 129

"Dr. Sedgwick," Dan McGrew, and Putzi Hanfstaengl ... 131

The OSS File on Hitler ... 138

W. H. Auden's Contribution ... 142

Klaus Richter Contributes a Cover ... 144

Visiting Professor at Texas and Voorhees ... 146

Soviet Russia by Bus: *Who Knows?* ... 151

Oxford: *"I'm Afraid I Must Battel You"* and Two Historians ... 155

Emergency Room, Radcliffe Infirmary … 160

In Pursuit of the Kaiser at Doorn … 162

Dr. Johnson and My Tapestry … 166

Tel Aviv, L.A. Rams, and Jerusalem … 168

Filmmaking in Alaska … 172

March in Portal, Arizona … 175

Lake Temagami and Polar Bears … 177

David Frost Interview with David Irving:
"Hitler Was Not an Anti-Semite" … 181

The Making of *Kaiser and Führer* … 184

"Man or Circumstance?" … 186

"Change or Continuity?" and a Harvard Seminar … 189

Objectivity, Sincerity, and the Historian … 192

"What Actually Happened" … 195

Similarities and Differences … 197

Operation Barbarossa: *"The World Will Hold Its Breath"* … 209

"War with the United States Was Illogical" … 211

"Our Greatest Enemy Is the Jew, the Eternal Jew" … 213

Kaiser and Führer in Two World Wars … 217

"The Resolve to Strike Was Always within Me" … 219

Psychological Dimensions … 221

Limitations of Psychology … 225

L'envoi: *"Where Do You Keep Your Mops?"* … 227

"Let's Stop This Chickenshit" … 234

"Williams in Oxford" … 236

Anne's Illness and Death … 237

PREFACE

Academic processions tend to be solemn, stodgy parades of colorfully gowned professors. This particular academic's procession will be neither solemn nor stodgy. The color will be provided by the variety of people and places I have encountered and by my efforts as a historian to deal with the careers and the intractable personalities of Kaiser Wilhelm II and Adolf Hitler.

R. G. L. W.
Sweetwood
Williamstown
18 February 1999

"Five coffees and one beer!"

FIVE COFFEES AND ONE BEER

In the spring of 1949, shortly after I had earned my doctorate from Harvard by the sweat of my Frau, I was invited to visit Williams College to be interviewed for an opening in the history department.

The position was an assistant professorship at the then unheard-of annual salary of $4,000. Anne and I agreed that that would be all the money we would ever need in our married life. I had finished at Harvard. I had no other prospects. We had a three-year-old son, and Anne was heavily pregnant. I needed that job. With nervous anticipation I took the train to Williamstown in the northwest corner of Massachusetts to be "looked over."

(At a farewell reception a proper Bostonian lady said to me, "I hear you are going out west to be interviewed for a position." When I replied "Well, I am going out to Williamstown," she said, "Yes, that's what I understand.")

The interview was an elaborate process. I met members of the department; I delivered a trial lecture and responded to questions. I was taken for a drive through the glorious Berkshire hills, I met with clean-shaven and haircutted white gentlemanly students in tweed jackets, button-down shirts with rep-striped ties, chinos, and white buck shoes, and I was invited to a fraternity house for dinner replete with cama-raderie, candlelight, and college songs. That night I slept in the Faculty House — private bath, two heavy, purple (the college color) silk dressing gowns (one large, one small), two pairs of purple kid slippers (large and small), and breakfast served to my order. Everyone was friendly; I was impressed. I liked everything about the place and thought I was doing rather well.

But the big hurdle would come when I met with President James Phinney Baxter III and the awesome Committee on Appointments and Promotions. Promptly at the appointed hour of 9:15 A.M., I met the president and the committee in his big office. President Baxter was a hearty, pear-shaped, energetic man with a voice like a Maine foghorn. (His secretary of many years recalled that one day when she told a waiting faculty member that the roar coming from the president's private office was Mr. Baxter talking to Washington, the visitor asked, "Why doesn't he use the telephone?")

The morning of my interview was a lovely, very warm day in May. Mr. Baxter was expansive. "It's too nice a day to meet here," he roared. "Let's all go down on the Street and have a drink at Mike's." (The Street was Spring Street, *the* commercial avenue of Williamstown; Mike's turned out to be a greasy spoon.)

The committee of three elected faculty members representing the three academic divisions (arts, social studies and sciences) was joined by the dean of the College. When we were seated around a large table, Baxter turned to me and asked heartily, "Well, Waite, what are you drinking?"

Since it was 9:30 in the morning, I didn't really want to drink anything. But I was afraid these sophisticates might be ordering double martinis, so I thought I'd better play it safe: "I'd like a beer, please."

President Baxter raised his eyebrows and asked, "A what? Did you say a *beer?*" That was a bit off-putting, but I was stuck with my decision. I said firmly, "Yes, sir, a beer."

Mr. Baxter called Mike over and gave his order: *"Five coffees and one beer!"*

Right then, I knew I had goofed badly. Convinced that the members of the committee were asking themselves what kind of lush they were interviewing, I called Anne that night and told her I had blown it. She laughed, told me to relax, I had probably done OK. As usual, she was right. I got the job.

The Williams hiring episode was a turning point in my life. It was both the culmination of a series of youthful experiences and the beginning of a career that included a variety of oddball episodes, culminating in my serious interest in Wilhelm II and Adolf Hitler, two men who were responsible for the two most important events of the twentieth century.

• • • • •

Let's start at the beginning. I was born on a kitchen table in a Canadian village during a world-class blizzard at 53 below zero without benefit of doctor or midwife. I grew up in a loving family presided over by a quiet but indomitable mother and a wondrously wacky, pun-loving father who was a Methodist preacher in prairie towns of Manitoba. In Swan River I helped a Mountie stable his horse and he let me fire his revolver. My brother and I rode many miles with Dukhobors (Old Believers who were religious refugees from Russia) in their bobsled and stayed overnight in their village. I memorized Robert W. Service by the yard. Indeed, if I had not known the words of "The Shooting of Dan McGrew," I never would have been able to interview the strange Harvard graduate who became one of Adolf Hitler's henchmen.

I lived on my own and worked my way through high school in a rural Minnesota town washing dishes, clerking at JC Penney Co., and serving as gardener and houseboy to a wealthy widow. I also played football badly and very nearly murdered a good friend.

To attend Macalester College in St. Paul, I poured cement for grain elevators in South Dakota, stripped bluegrass in Minnesota, shoveled iron ore in open pit mines of the Mesabi Range, and earned money in a carnival sleeping alongside the corpse of John Wilkes Booth. But more about all that later.

I had an undistinguished career in the Army during World War II and married the wonderful girl I had met on a blind date in 1943. After getting my doctorate on the GI Bill of Rights, I taught European history for three years at Harvard College and then for forty happy years at

Williams College. During leaves and sabbaticals away from Williams, I also learned a great deal from teaching at the University of Texas in Austin and at an all-black college in South Carolina, as well as from serving as a Senior Associate Member of an Oxford University college.

With sabbaticals providing the time and Messrs. Guggenheim and Fulbright the funds, I pursued two special interests that became passions and eventually books: *The Psychopathic God: Adolf Hitler* (1977; 1993, paperback) and *Kaiser and Führer: A Comparative Study of Personality and Politics* (1998).

Like many historians, I am keenly interested in the role of personalities in history. It is obvious to me that any attempt to understand the past 200 years requires an exploration of how the personalities of such people as Napoleon, Otto von Bismarck, Woodrow Wilson, Franklin Roosevelt, Wilhelm II, and Adolf Hitler influenced the course of events. But in recent years many historians have not shared this view, arguing that historical movements and events are primarily caused by social and economic forces. For these historians, the personalities of national leaders are of minor importance.

In 1983, for example, Harvard University hosted an international conference of scholars on the fiftieth anniversary of the Nazi seizure of power. Dozens of excellent papers were read, but not one of them dealt with the part played by Adolf Hitler. To my mind that was really like trying to stage *Hamlet* without the prince of Denmark, or the *Hunchback of Notre Dame* without Quasimodo. Of course economic and social forces help determine history. But so do individuals. Jesus made a difference, and so did Martin Luther and Mahatma Gandhi and Vladimir Lenin. And so did the two German rulers who, twice in the twentieth century, drove their countries to ruin and the world to war.

As I became more knowledgeable about the strange personalities of these two men, I became aware that I very much needed the help of psychopathologists to understand them. Traditional historians, however, have taken a dim view of this approach. Indeed, the late A. J. P. Taylor, a well-known British traditionalist, told me that he "totally disagreed" with everything I was doing. And in his farewell lecture, which packed

4

the Sheldonian Theatre at Oxford, the distinguished historian announced his own credo. Disdaining interest in irrational forces, he asserted that his personal interpretations of important historical figures had "relied entirely upon my greatest gift as an historian: old-fashioned common sense."

As I see it, common sense invites us to accept, rather than reject, the contributions psychologists have made to our understanding. Professor Taylor's — or anyone else's — common sense cannot account for the Kaiser's insistence on alienating the very people he needed to cultivate; nor can it account for the sheer *senselessness* of Hitler's Holocaust. Nor can common sense tell us why both of these rulers persisted in acting in ways least likely to succeed and most likely to defeat their own political or military purposes.

Psychology can help us fathom human motivation, but only up to a point. It cannot explain why the Kaiser enjoyed humiliating old men or inflicting pain on young women or ridiculing those who — like himself — were physically handicapped. Nor can it account for the overwhelming personal magnetism of Adolf Hitler. Nor are psychologists interested in exploring the dimensions of evil that characterized his conduct. Indeed, the very word "evil" cannot be found in the indexes of standard journals of psychopathology.

So I came to the conclusion that psychology could help me in my historical research, but that's all it could do. Which is to say I agree with what Thomas Aquinas said hundreds of years ago. In discussing the power of human reason he concluded that "it is essential, but not sufficient."

I found psychology particularly useful in comparing Kaiser and Führer. I discovered that they were at once remarkably alike and strikingly different: Both were seriously mentally disturbed, both had been battered children, both were talented politicians who committed monumental political blunders, both were lovers of Richard Wagner and both tried to write operas; both were incessant talkers and both were adequate watercolorists; both were racist anti-Semites — many years before the Nazis came to power, the Kaiser remarked that "the best way to handle the Jews would be gas." Both rulers enjoyed childish games: the Kaiser

5

liked to play tag; the Führer to see how fast he could get undressed and jump into bed.

Yet there was one overriding difference between the two rulers: Hitler was evil; Wilhelm Hohenzollern — for all his many faults — was not.

• • • • •

These memories, then, will include both lighthearted episodes and the culmination of my academic procession: a serious and reflective concern for a better understanding of the personalities and careers of two historic figures.

FATHER MEETS MOTHER
AND NO FIREWATER

Of course my personal procession really began with many generations' worth of ancestral genes but, more immediately, with my English mother and father.

Father was born and raised in Lincoln, where for centuries Waites had been stonecutters in Lincoln Cathedral, until Grandfather, noting how many in his family had died early from silicosis, broke the chain and apprenticed my father to a cabinetmaker.

Sometime during his mid-twenties my father had a transforming religious experience, joined the Wesleyan Methodist Church, and became a lay preacher. His ordination picture shows a handsome, robust young man with a grimly determined chin — but also with a twinkle in his eye that, happily, he never lost.

One Sunday evening he preached in the Methodist chapel. In attendance was my future mother, who was then mistress of a school for young ladies. This Miss Alice Carter and my father fell in love and became engaged. When he was suddenly "called" to a church in rural Ontario, it was agreed that he would go out alone to see the lay of the bush and, if it seemed manageable, Mother would go out and join him. They would be married in his new Canadian parish.

On a lovely June evening in 1911, after Dad had preached his final sermon in England, one of his parishioners, a little old woman in black straw hat and gray shawl, approached my mother. "I 'ear tell that Miss Carter will be a-leavin' to go to Canada to marry our young preacher." When Miss Carter assured her that that was, indeed, the case, she

7

replied — in words Mother later loved to recall — "You know, m'dear, 'e does so remind me of my 'enry, what 'anged hisself."

From Canada Dad wrote romantic love letters on birchbark, which my mother treasured until her death more than twenty-five years later. She arrived in Ontario in the late summer of 1911 armed with a "muff pistol," a tiny derringer that she had purchased in Paris. It had been designed to discourage unwanted male advances. Mother thought it would also be useful in fending off moose and bear.

My mother was a small woman with lovely long auburn hair, transparent skin, unflappable disposition, and a smile that lit many a room. But when her hazel eyes flashed, there was cold steel behind them, and it meant that no nonsense would be tolerated. Anyone could tell that she had been a schoolmarm and when she had given an order to an unruly student, she had been obeyed.

One bitterly cold night just before Christmas, she was alone in the little cottage that served as a manse in northern Ontario. My father had left to be with a dying parishioner. Suddenly Mother was startled by a loud pounding that shook the front door. She opened it to be confronted by an enormous Ojibway who growled, "I am cold, gimme firewater!"

Mother smiled radiantly, graciously invited him to come in. "No firewater. You sit there by the fire." The Indian stepped forward, sucked in his breath, puffed out his chest, took a menacing step toward my mother, and roared, "I said, *firewater!*"

Mother did not budge. She drew herself up to her full five feet, two inches, her eyes flashed, and she snapped, "I said, *no firewater!*" She pointed to a chair by the fire and said firmly, "You sit right down there. I will bring you something better than firewater." The Indian grunted. But he sat down.

Mother brought him a mug of hot cocoa and a large slice of the fruitcake she had baked for Christmas. The Ojibway grunted again and said, "Heap good! More, please?" Mother refilled his mug, brought one for herself, and sat down beside him. After about fifteen uneasy minutes, the Indian gave a final grunt, grinned, and departed.

When Dad returned, my trembling mother collapsed in his arms and sobbed out her story. He told her, as he often did, that she was "a brick" — that was his highest word of praise. ("Piker!" expressed ultimate contempt.)

Dad liked to recall the day he was out hiking with a newly arrived Scots visitor. An enormous animal with immense antlers came crashing through the bush. The Scot exclaimed, "Hoot, mon, and what's *that?*" My father told him it was a moose. "Ach, mon," the Scot cried in alarm, "if that's a Canadian mouse, I dinna care to see one of your *cats!*"

My Canadian Boyhood

In Canada in the years following the Great War, an ecumenical movement sought to form a union of Protestant denominations into the United Church of Canada, or UCC, which doctrinally is parallel to the United Church of Christ (UCC) in the United States. My father was instrumental in helping form UCC churches in the rural villages of Manitoba.

That is how I arrived on the scene in the prairie village of Cartwright, Manitoba, during a howling blizzard on a night that was 53 degrees below zero (no "chill factor" computed). The village midwife could not make it through the storm. There was no doctor. My mother gave me birth on the kitchen table, near the wood-burning range, with help from Father and my eight-year-old sister, Stella.

But all that is hearsay. My memory starts after we arrived in Franklin, a remote village then — and probably now — of perhaps 200 people with one street, a one-room elementary school, Freeman's General Store (groceries, dry goods, confections cum post office cum hand-pumped gas), one church, a skating rink, and some two dozen houses.

We lived in a sprawling, drafty old manse. We had a small barn, two horses (Betty and Jock), a cow, two pigs, chickens, and a half-acre vegetable garden. I can see my father now, naked to the waist, exuberantly hacking the weeds, his powerful body glistening in the sun. I can still smell the olive oil he rubbed onto his skin — we had never heard of "suntan lotion." I often wondered why he was the only member of our pink-toned family who could get a tan. My older brother, Greg, and I helped with the weeding. My mother and sisters, Stella and Nancy, put up dozens of jars of vegetables against the long winter months when there were no fresh vegetables in Freeman's General Store.

One winter the snowfall was so heavy and the winds so strong that our little stable was completely covered with snow. Dad cut a hole in the slanting roof and lowered feed for the chickens and the livestock. We four Waite children, as well as neighboring kids, suddenly found ourselves blessed with the only hill in town. We spent happy hours hauling our wooden sleds to the top of the barn and sliding down into our backyard.

In one moment of glorious exuberance, I yelled, "Wow, I'm going like hell!" Just as I uttered that awful word, I looked up and saw my reverend father. I was desperately afraid that he had heard me. I suffered pangs of guilt and wanted to punish myself for the terrible thing I had done. I remember going to the compost heap by the back door of our house and looking for a piece of broken glass so that I could cut my hand. Luckily, I couldn't find one.

I was usually a happy kid, but throughout my early childhood I was plagued by feelings of self-reproach. Once my sister Stella saw me sitting morosely by myself and said, "Bobbie, don't sulk!" When I asked her what that word meant, she said, "Feeling sorry for yourself." I remember thinking that she didn't understand at all. It was just the opposite: I was not feeling sorry for myself, but for the people who had to live with such a wicked little boy.

In looking back, I have no idea where such bleak feelings came from. They were certainly not inspired by a morally censorious father. But I must have thought so at the time of the "like hell" incident. This shows how little I understood about my father's conception of morality or religion. I remember the enormous relief I felt a few days later when I heard him use the same word in an equally nontheological context and then ask, "Would anyone not in Holy Orders care to say some other appropriate words?"

Further enlightenment about my father's religious faith came later, when I was burdened by some terrible sin or other that I was sure I had committed. Dad took me aside and said, "Bob, I know that something is bothering you badly. I don't know what it is, but I want you to remember what I am going to tell you now: Our God is the God of love. He will always love you and forgive you for whatever you have done. And so will I." I have not forgotten those words. I also remember his saying that God had a lively sense of humor, adding, "How else could He put up with us?"

VISITING THE DUKHOBORS

My father had a "mission parish" much farther north, which he visited twice a year, once in winter, once in summer. To make the winter trip, he wore an enormous bearskin coat, gauntlets and hat, red-plaid mackinaw pants, two pairs of heavy woolen socks knitted by my mother, and felt boots. A charcoal foot warmer and bearskin rug completed his equipment. Betty, with horse blanket and steaming nostrils, was harnessed to the tinkling-belled cutter and they were off.

Father returned with absorbing tales of lumber camps. For instance, I remember him telling us that one night after a dinner of caribou, with kitchen knives and cooking forks shoved to the side, he watched the men play a high-stakes game of poker. Suddenly one lumberjack grabbed a carving fork and slammed it through an opponent's hand, pinning it to the table, saying quietly, "Jack, if the ace of spades ain't under that hand, I'll apologize."

His return from northern trips was a big event in our lives. I can still smell his steaming bearskin coat as he hugged his children while thawing out over the hot-air radiator. And I can hear the contented sound of hungry teeth chewing the fried potatoes and onions saved for him from our Sunday roast.

Our source of heat was a voracious wood furnace in the dirt cellar. On Saturday afternoons my brother and I would watch two friendly Dukhobors unload cords of birch logs — three dollars a cord — from their bobsled. Greg and I helped pile the sweet-smelling logs in enormous neat piles outside our back door. Dad sometimes let us ride partway home with the Dukhobors in their empty sled until we met another sled filled with logs coming toward us from Franklin. One of the drivers taught us rollicking Russian folk songs that are, I'm sorry to say, long gone from my mind.

The Russians were skilled axmen. I remember when one of them took a two-foot log, six inches in diameter, set it on its end, and placed his steel Ingersol pocket watch in the center. Then, with his razor-sharp double-bitted ax, he split the wood in two-inch slices from the periphery toward the center, splitting round and round so precisely that he left the watch standing on a pedestal with no more than a thin rim of wood around it.

When I was seven, I think, Father took my brother and me in the buggy on one of his summer visits to his remote northern parish. En route we stayed overnight in parishioners' farmhouses. One time we stayed at a Dukhobor settlement, where we were welcomed by the patriarch, a kindly, spade-bearded giant with incredibly blue eyes and a friendly smile. I have not forgotten the warmth of our welcome or the rich fragrance of freshly baked Russian bread as it was drawn from outdoor clay ovens. I remember, too, the Evensong service and the deep bass resonance of the patriarch's voice as he led the hauntingly beautiful Russian hymns, and the serenity evoked by his prayers, whose words we could not understand but whose spirit we found deeply moving.

My Father's Parodies and Puns

Father liked to compose parodies of poems and songs. To the tune of "It ain't gonna rain no more, no more, it ain't gonna rain no more, so how in the heck can I wash my neck, if it ain't gonna rain no more?" My father sang in his lusty baritone:

Oh, a man lay down by a sewer
And by the sewer he died,
And at the coroner's inquest
They called it sewer-side.

He composed a melancholy ode to Rosie O'Grady:

Sweet Rosie O'Grady, she was a seamstress by birth,
But she got tired of living and decided to leave this earth.
So she swallowed her tape line, but dying by inches was hard,
So she went out in the alley and she died there by the yard.

One day Mother had cooked an unusually tough old chicken, which my father memorialized in words she ultimately forgave:

Oh, this old cock was there
When they built the Tower of Babel
It was raised by Cain and Abel
And housed in old Noah's stable.

15

All the shots that were fired on the field of Waterloo
Could not penetrate or dislocate
This elongated, iron-plated, brazen crested, steel-vested
Cockal-doodle-doo.

At supper table Father would ask, "Bobbie, what moral lesson does a weathercock on a church steeple suggest?" When neither I nor anyone else at the table responded, my father answered his own question with a triumphant grin: "'Tis a vane thing to a spire."

I had started school in Franklin. I remember drawing a birdhouse and proudly taking home other objets d'art. For I had been inspired by the finest teacher I have ever known. She taught all eight grades in the one-room school. From the first day I knew she was a genius. My mother looked at one of my contributions to abstract art, said it was very nice, and asked what on earth it was. I paid high tribute to my mentor: *"I* don't know what it is, Mommie, and *you* don't know. But *Miss Armstrong* knows."

As in all Canadian towns, the recreational center in winter was the village rink. A long rectangle with a corrugated iron roof, it contained at its center another rectangle divided into two squares. One square was reserved for the Curling Club.

The sport of curling had been popular in Scotland for more than 300 years before it was adopted by Canadians as a national winter sport. It is played with heavy, round, polished granite stones that have handles on the top. The rules are like those for lawn bowling. Two teams, usually with four players each, take part. Each player "curls," that is, slides his forty-two-pound stone along the ice, using the handles to set it spinning slowly to either the left or the right as it slides on its way toward the target, or "tee," about thirty-five yards distant. This target consists of multicolored concentric circles with a red bull's-eye center, dyed in the ice. The object is to curl the stones closer to the center than one's opponents.

An important feature of the game is sweeping the ice with long-bristled brooms. Two players are designated "sweeps" who follow the directions of their captain, the "skip." By vigorous sweeping in front of the stone, they can make it travel farther and faster toward the "tee" or cause it to knock the opponent's stone out of contention.

I can still hear excited voices crying, "Sweep! Sweep! Swe-e-e-p 'er up!" I still see overweight men with red faces, wearing Scot tam-o'-shanters, puffing and sweeping like mad in front of curling stones. I remember one set of stones with Old Dutch Cleanser girls glazed on their granite sides. They whirled merrily around, chasing nonexistent dirt and knocking opponents' stones out of the way.

The other square was reserved for hockey, which all Canadian boys began playing at the age of five or six. In Franklin we were not permitted to play when the thermometer registered more than 40 degrees below zero Fahrenheit. We thought it silly that our parents were afraid we would freeze our lungs. But we rejoiced that the 40-below cutoff also meant we couldn't walk the half mile to school.

The oval space outside the central rectangle of the rink was reserved for everyone else, those who skated around and around while a windup gramophone played over and over again "The Blue Danube" and "The Skater's Waltz."

Each year in Franklin we had a winter carnival, with prizes for the fastest skaters and the best costumes. One year Greg and I went as Chinese brothers. Mother dressed us in kimonos made out of her colorful old aprons. Since our hair color — light brown and lighter blond — and our delicate Saxon complexion lent no verisimilitude to our roles, Mother braided her black cotton stockings into queues to cover our heads and dyed our skin with butter coloring. We won first prize, a quarter of a dollar for each of us! Never had we had so much money in our young lives. Although we remained the color of daffodils for at least a week, the glory and the cash made it all worthwhile.

My mother, who had been active in student dramatics at Aberystwyth College in Wales, and two other women formed the Cartwright Theatre Club. They rented an old granary where my father helped build the stage. My sisters and their friends painted posters that my brother and I nailed up all over the village.

The play we advertised was *Caste,* a satire of the snobbery of English officers and their wives during the British Raj of India. It was not an entirely appropriate play for a rural Canadian village, where snobbery was unknown and the climate frigid. But it was a huge success in Franklin.

Thanks to these plays, village people and farmers, many for the first time in their lives, were brought together on the stage to perform before family and friends. The granary was packed for every performance.

THE DEATH OF GRANNY WAITE

Grandmother Waite came over to live with us in Franklin after her husband died in Lincoln of "stonemason's disease." Three daughters and a son had died early deaths from tuberculosis, leaving my father as her only surviving relative. I remember her as a quiet, frail little woman dressed in black, smelling faintly of lavender and having no teeth.

Apart from her thin gold wedding ring, her only ornament was a lovely little cameo, a classical Grecian profile, which she wore on a narrow black ribbon around her neck. Her demeanor was rather stern, but she was invariably kind to her grandchildren. She told us about her childhood in England, where at the age of thirteen she had been sent to earn her living as a scullery maid for one of the great lords of the realm. She was docked a week's wages one day because, while toiling up a hill with two heavy water buckets, she had failed to put them down to curtsy to the *empty* carriage of Lord Whozit.

A devout Methodist, she listened to our evening prayers and sang hymns to us as lullabies in a soft alto voice: "There were ninety and nine that safely lay in the shelter of the fold . . ." While singing another hymn she saw that I was upset by the phrase "shadows of the evening *steal* across the sky." She changed it to *"creep* across the sky," and I was comforted. My own religious beliefs were greatly influenced by Granny's prayers, her simple faith, and the serenity and quiet dignity of her life and death.

She had been with us for about two years when she suffered a severe stroke and lay in bed for weeks almost totally paralyzed and speechless.

On the evening she died, the family gathered around her bed. I remember looking up at the faces of my mother and father. I was puzzled to see that they were crying but they were also smiling through their tears. Father asked us to hold hands as he led us in family prayers. Each of us in turn told her how much we loved her. I remember a warm feeling of loving my whole family.

Then Granny suddenly sat straight up in her bed and sang clearly in her lovely voice, "Nearer my God to Thee, nearer to Thee. . ." She then dropped back and died with a quiet smile on her face.

It was the first time I had seen anyone die. Death was a great mystery to me, but not at all frightening. Indeed, it brought our family closer together.

MY FIRST LOVE AFFAIR

At five I fell in love with Birdy Bennett, by far the prettiest little girl in Franklin. Precocious, too. She could undo buttons better than I could, and she taught me to play her special version of Doctor: "I'll let you see mine, if you let me see yours." She seemed gratified with my contribution to the game; I remember feeling gypped.

For Birdy Bennett I started to enter a life of crime. For Birdy I stole a chocolate from Freeman's General Store. My father found out about it, gave me a stern lecture on thievery, handed me a five-cent piece, ordered me to go to Mr. Freeman, confess my guilt, tell him I was sorry, that I would never, ever, do it again, and give him the nickel. I tried to explain to my father that all I had taken was one single chocolate, not a whole five-cent chocolate bar. But he would have none of it. I did what I was told because I respected my father, but also because I wanted to stay on friendly terms with Mr. Freeman. He always gave me an extra scoop of ice cream in the five-cent vanilla cone that I shared with Birdy and her snivel-nosed, bleary-eyed, drooling Boston bulldog named Buster — named to honor the brand of shoes she wore.

Both self-interest and gallantry inspired me to arrange the sequence of our licks: first Birdy, then me, then Buster, then Birdy. . . .

CHRISTMAS IN FRANKLIN
AND THE ENGLISH BOX

In Franklin we had "proper English Christmases" that began after morning prayers with a piece of pork pie that, by Father's instructions, "must be stone cold." Then we opened our meager and mostly handmade gifts, followed by family games of Simon Says Thumbs Up, Hunt the Thimble, Charades, and Kingdoms (animal, mineral, or vegetable?). Finally, a huge dinner of goose and plum pudding brought in flaming with forbidden brandy (which we must not report to our friends) and with crackers to pop and paper hats to wear while singing Christmas carols.

When I was about five, with the help of my older sisters I laboriously composed a long letter to Santa Claus, which Nancy promptly threw into the kitchen range. I was hurt and furious. Nor was I completely reassured by her telling me that my letter was not really destroyed; the only way Santa could get my message was by reading it written in the smoke coming out of our chimney. Since at that moment the smoke was being swirled about by a gale-force wind that was rattling the storm windows and shaking the house, I started entertaining serious doubts about the very existence of the prospective recipient of any smoke signals.

I was particularly disappointed that Christmas. I had played with an ocarina in a parishioner's house, and I loved its sweet and mellow sound. I set my heart on getting one for Christmas. But either because I could not explain what I wanted or none was attainable, or my father could not afford it, what I got for Christmas was a tin kazoo. I suppose it was good for my character to express gratitude.

Every year at Christmas we looked forward to getting the absolutely marvelous "English box," a large carton whose wondrous contents had an indescribable, mysterious odor, possibly from spices in the ship's hold. The box contained lavish gifts from my mother's well-to-do family, who thought kindly of their poor Canadian relatives. One Christmas my brother and I received realistic, bright-yellow tin Aston-Martin roadsters. I remember winding them up as tightly as we dared, aiming them carefully and watching them zip clear across the kitchen linoleum floor — when they didn't crash into the wood-burning kitchen range.

The most wonderful present I ever received came from my Uncle Bob. Somehow he had managed to acquire an official London bobby's whistle. When my father told me that with such a whistle I could fend off nefarious international spies and robbers, I spent Christmas, and succeeding days, blowing it officially up one side of the village street and down the other. My father was right: Not one nefarious international criminal dared show his face in Franklin, Manitoba, while I and my whistle were there. I still have that whistle.

About that time I got my first pair of glasses. They were horn-rimmed and — combined with my curly, very blond hair, round face, and serious mien — made me look a bit like an owl. This, and their awareness of my penchant for big words, prompted my sisters to give me my family name, "Prof." I now recall with some embarrassment a demonstration of my seven-year-old verbal virtuosity. Our family had been invited to a prosperous parishioner's house for Harvest Home (Thanksgiving) dinner. When the kindly hostess asked me if I would like another piece of pumpkin pie, I replied, with prose carefully prepared in advance for such an occasion: "No thank you, madam, I am completely surensified [a word of my own invention]. Any more of your delectable cuisine might prove obnoxious to my rather fastidious palate." Mrs. Widlake was flabbergasted; my mother was appalled; my father guffawed.

My Rescue at Rock Lake

Every August of my childhood was spent at Rock Lake, Manitoba, where my father had joined with other UCC ministers to establish and maintain a church camp. The camp was primitive, but for us kids it was at least the equivalent of Disneyland. We had outdoor toilets, galvanized-tin-roofed men's and women's dormitories with straw mattresses, and a common dining room and kitchen, no electricity, no running water, and of course no TV, but unlimited swimming and lots of new friends. And each of us was given the princely spending allowance of five cents *every day!* How to invest our daily munificence was the topic of lively conversation as we walked a mile and a half around the lake to Avery's Boat Delivery (live bait, fishing tackle, rented outboard motors, groceries, and confections). My sisters recklessly blew their allowance on vanilla or strawberry ice-cream cones. But my brother and I prolonged our pleasure with a more enduring investment: an entire package of Chicklets, Wrigley's PKs, which seemed named especially for us "preacher's kids." I had not heard that expression again until some fifty years later in London, when David Frost, the son of a Methodist clergyman, welcomed me at lunch by noting that we had something in common. "We're both PKs."

At Rock Lake we became very friendly with the Dodd family. Harry, a gaunt, hatchet-faced but pleasant man with a crippled hand, came from Yorkshire and was minister of a UCC church in some large town in Manitoba. He and my father had great fun talking in heavy Yorkshire and Lincolnshire accents. Jenny Dodd and my mother became lifelong friends. The Dodds had a daughter who suffered from Down syndrome. Their patient, good-humored, and tender relationship with their handicapped daughter gave me insight into the dimensions of human love.

I remember stormy nights at Rock Lake with thunder rolling, lightning crashing over the storm-tossed lake, and rain pounding against the metal roof while our fathers told wondrous ghost stories as we lay safe and dry in our fragrant straw beds. In the early morning, the fragrant odor of a distant skunk lingered over the dormitory.

One day I needed badly to go to the toilet and was dismayed to find that the men's outhouse was occupied. Desperate, I used the women's. Terrified that the kids would see me leaving the "Ladies'," I opened the door a crack to see approaching the enormous form of my deliverer, Mrs. Blanchard, a woman of gargantuan girth, golden heart, and total understanding of a terrified seven-year-old boy's distress. She said jovially, "Don't worry. We can fool them. You hide under my apron; I'm so big that no one will notice an extra bulge or two. Just walk slowly and I'll keep in step with you. No one will see you leaving the Ladies'." It worked to perfection. I could find no adequate way to thank her, but it is one of the kindest things anyone has ever done for me.

Getting to Rock Lake was, if not "half the fun," at least a good part of it. After our Model T had been loaded beyond its gunwales, my father led us in brief family prayers. And as we entered the open gravel road, from whatever town we were then living in, we sang our family hymn: "Now thank we all our God, with hearts and hands and voices. . ." En route we played guessing games such as Kingdoms and a game my mother invented that we called Horse Tennis. When one of us saw a horse, she or he would shout, "Fifteen love!" When someone saw a team of horses — which in those days was quite often — "Thirty-fifteen!" If the first person then saw another team, "Forty-thirty!" A white horse counted double.

We had a special treat one summer when I was about five. While going home from the lake, we stopped off at the big town of Brandon, Manitoba, to see our first cowboy movie. I was enthralled. Armed with a toy cap pistol, I got into the spirit of the thing and started to help my hero, Tom Mix — or was it Ken Maynard? — by shooting the bad guys in black hats. The manager was a nice man. He came down the aisle and told me that he didn't like the bad guys either, but he didn't want them shot from the audience. Besides, he was sure that Tom Mix would be able to take care of them. Then he confiscated my weapon but told me I could have it back at the end of the movie.

Rock Lake came back into my life some fifty years later. Anne and I had flown out to Seattle, where I gave a talk to the Seattle Williams Alumni Association. We decided to return to Williamstown by crossing Canada on Via Rail from Vancouver to Montreal. The month was February and the previous night there had been a fifteen-inch snowfall in British Columbia and Alberta. We woke up to see the sun rising over the sheer glory of the snow-laden trees in the high Canadian Rockies.

Sitting near us in the observation car were two Canadian farming couples. Directly behind us were two Mennonites: he in dark suit and tieless white shirt, she in white bonnet and apron. Across the aisle from the Mennonites sat another farmer and his wife. They were obviously rather well off. Both couples said that they usually went to Florida during the month of February, but since the Canadian dollar was so weak they thought it would be fun, for the first time, to take a pleasure trip "clear across Canada." When they exchanged information about their lives, my ears really pricked up when the Mennonite said his farm was near a little village that "nobody ever heard of: Franklin, Manitoba." He went on to say that during the summer, he often led devotions at their Mennonite church camp on Rock Lake, which was on the shore opposite a UCC camp. I turned around, introduced myself and said I would like to ask him a couple of questions: Was there still a Freeman's General Store in Franklin? Was Avery's Boat Delivery still operating on Rock Lake? I do not remember ever seeing a more surprised look on a person's face. There followed a pleasant and, for me, rewarding discussion about Franklin and our religious faiths. I forgot to ask him, darn it, if he knew what Birdy Bennett was doing.

GRANDMOTHER CARTER, ENCOUNTER WITH A MOUNTIE, AND KING TUT'S TOMB

When I was eight our family moved from Franklin farther north and west to Swan River, a larger town of about 800 people, the Klondike gold rush of the '90s still fresh in many old-timers' memories. My father was a fan of Robert W. Service and memorized his doggerel by the yard. I, too, learned by heart "Ballad of the Cremation of Sam McGee" and "The Shooting of Dan McGrew":

> *A bunch of the boys were whooping it up in the Malamute Saloon;*
> *The kid that handles the music box was hitting a jag-time tune;*
> *Back of the bar in a solo game sat Dangerous Dan McGrew,*
> *And watching his luck was his Light o' Love, the lady that's known as Lou.*
> *When out of the night which was 50 below, and into the din and the glare,*
> *There stumbled a miner fresh from the creeks, dog-dirty and loaded for bear.*

Many years later in Germany, while doing research on Adolf Hitler, I had reason to thank Dan McGrew for those lines. Stay tuned.

In Swan River I met my boyhood sports hero, Max Stewart, the finest athlete in town. And a daredevil. In April when the ice was breaking up like thunder and shaking the steel bridge over the Swan River, he would run across the swaying five-inch-wide handrail to the cheers of the spectators. Max always won the shotput and "tossing the caber" (the Scottish sport of heaving a telephone pole backward over your left shoulder). Watching the 100-yard dash, I stood at the finish line cheering him on to victory. I remember smelling his pungently perspiring

As soon as we heard a deep grunt of satisfaction,
Greg jumped onto the extended end of the plank.

body as he passed right by me. How wonderful it would be, I thought, if I could smell like Max Stewart when I grew up.

An even greater hero arrived at our door one spring when Constable Browning, a real live Royal Canadian Mounted Policeman, dismounted his magnificent chestnut steed and asked if we could accommodate him in our sprawling old manse and barn his horse for the night. For he was on the trail of a dangerous criminal who had been sighted north of our town. Could we? Wow! In all his crimson-coated glory, this friendly giant, at least eight feet tall, leaned down to shake my hand. (Note: As an expert in these matters has pointed out to me, the constable's tunic that day was probably a working uniform of drab khaki, crimson tunics being reserved for dress parade. But my boyhood memory insists it was crimson when he called on us.)

In the barn my brother got oats for his enormous horse and I held its bridle with its shining pure-silver bit. The biggest thrill came when Constable Browning let us hold his heavy service revolver and we went behind the barn, where he let us each fire a shot into some bales of hay. To top it off, he gave each of us a shiny quarter for our help with his horse. I hadn't had a whole quarter since winning first prize in the Cartwright winter carnival.

Mr. Davidson was the meanest man in Swan River. He had the only apple tree in town, but he would never let us have any of its fruit. He even threatened to shoot us if we tried to pick up apples that had fallen to the ground. He preferred to let them rot. It was Mr. Davidson's custom after supper to "cross the yard" — a local euphemism for visiting the outhouse. One Halloween my brother, Greg, had an idea that was inspired. He and two older boys found a broad plank, which, from the rear of the privy, we stealthily pushed over the horizontal two-by-fours near the back of the structure. These would serve as a fulcrum for the plank, which extended about seven inches under Mr. Davidson's bottom. As soon as we heard a deep grunt of satisfaction, Greg jumped onto the extended end of the plank. As we raced away, we were delighted to hear screams of fury.

One of the toughest kids in Swan River was D. L. Sherbrook, a freckle-faced, red-headed fireball who would beat up anyone who called him by his right name. He insisted that we call him by his initials for very good reason. His mother had tried unsuccessfully for years, and finally, in her mid-forties, managed to give birth to her only child. She was so ecstatic about her good fortune that she had her son baptized Darling Lover. I can hear her shrill voice calling him to supper when we were in the midst of some exciting game: "Dar-ling Luh-ver!. . . Oh, Dar-ling Luh-ver Sherbrook, come to sup-per!" D. L. would glower belligerently at all of us, daring anyone to make any kind of comment.

The game we had been playing may well have been "Canadians vs. Germans," with the always-victorious Canadians triumphantly singing a song we considered clever and terribly daring: "Our soldiers went to war, our soldiers won, our soldiers stuck a bayonet up the Kaiser's —. Our soldiers went to war. . ."

Bridget O'Brien was a large, no-nonsense Irishwoman who helped my mother with spring housecleaning. When I was eight, she gave me a memorable lesson both in manners and in the effective use of descriptive nouns. One lovely morning I met her coming up our walk as I was on my way to school. I greeted her impudently in my broadest Irish brogue, "Well, if it is not Bridget O'Brien herself! The top o' the mornin' to ya, Bridget, me darlin'! The top o' the mornin'!"

She was not amused: "Top o' the morning, is it? If I have any more of your lip, you little pipsqueak, it will be the back of my hand to the front of your face!"

One summer Grandmother Carter and my aunts Stella and Dorothy came to visit us in Swan River. Grandmother's husband, who had been made prosperous by a Northampton brewery (which my grandmother did not like to mention) and a leather-goods business, had recently died.

I remember Grandmother Carter as a haughty woman who seldom smiled, wore many rings, and constantly sniffed smelling salts encased in a filigreed sterling-silver container. Our town's primitive sanitary facilities, the lack of sidewalks, and the swarms of ravenous mosquitoes did nothing to dissuade Grandmother from her conviction that her daughter

Alice had married "well beneath her station in life." She was appalled by Swan River.

Auntie Stella was a large, laughing, unmarried schoolmistress who brought us our first proper cricket bat. My father tried and failed to unravel the mysteries of cricket, but we had fun playing a simplified three-person version with a ball made from tightly wound rags.

Auntie Dorothy, a tall, handsome woman, had been deeply in love with a pleasant-faced young man whose picture she kept in a locket. After Grandfather Carter died, Grandmother announced that she needed Dorothy to care for her. The engagement was canceled. Dot was a great sport who wore handsome high leather boots and loved the outdoors. She had been the leader of a Girl Guide troop in England and helped my father set up Camp Craft Hollow, a rough church camp upstream on the river. The camp inspired one of my father's songs, which he sang lustily to the tune of "A Long, Long Trail A-winding":

There's a long green worm a-winding onto the roof of my tent,
And the morning whistle tells me that it's time I went.
There's the cold, cold water waiting for me to take my morning dip.
When I return, I'll find that worm upon my pillow slip.

One evening, while listening through the cold-air radiator in the upstairs hall to the grownup conversation in the parlor, I heard Grandmother, who was fond of "sweets," remark to her daughter, "Alice, tomorrow you shall make some fudge. If it turns out badly, the children may have a piece."

I also heard her telling the other grownups about the exploits of her late husband's "cousin," the late Howard Carter, who with Lord Carnarvon had recently (1922) made the sensational discovery of King Tut's tomb. I have no idea if Howard Carter was actually related to Grandfather Carter. He may have been a thirty-second cousin twice or thrice removed. Grandmother showed us several statuettes and sacred scarabs — the kind Grandfather could have picked up in a Cairo souvenir shop on one of his many solo trips to Greece, the Holy Land, and

Egypt. We were particularly intrigued with stories of "the curse of King Tut" — that anyone who entered his sacred tomb would suffer terrible punishment.

Some fifty years later, Anne and I joined an excursion up the Nile to the Valley of the Kings. Until the day we visited King Tut's empty tomb, I was the only one of the group who had not suffered a severe case of *mal d'étranger.* Then, upon leaving his tomb, I turned to Anne and remarked, "Well, you know, Tutankhamen-rah was really only a minor pharaoh." Minor pharaoh indeed! That night his dreadful pharaonic curse descended upon me. I had the runs for eight full days and nights.

But back to Swan River. The best — indeed, as I remember, the only — restaurant in town was Wong Lee's, where, as a special treat, my mother sometimes took the family for Sunday dinner after church. The food was delicious. I particularly liked to show off my skill with chopsticks, which I had been taught to use by a shell-shocked missionary who had stayed at our house for a year. One Saturday afternoon Greg and I stood on an apple box and looked through the kitchen window to see Mr. Lee putting the final touches on lemon meringue pies before putting them into the oven. He took a mouthful of milk and ejected a thin milken stream gently and delicately over the beaten egg whites so that the pies would brown in the oven. We were impressed with the artistry of his performance. Greg never forgave me for telling Mother about it, for we never visited Wong Lee's again.

My father's versifying spread through the family. For Mother's birthday one year, he had asked each of us to write her a poem. The lines penned by my sisters could have been copied from commercial birthday cards, if any had existed in Swan River during the 1920s. My effort has also been forgotten. But my brother's lived on in the family:

To My Mother

Who took me from my warm, warm cot
And put me on that cold, cold pot
Whether I needed to go or not
My mother!

WINNIPEG: ELECTRICITY, FLUSH TOILETS, AND PAVED ROADS

When I was nine, there was great excitement when my father received a "call" to be minister of a large UCC church in Winnipeg. It was a city of marvels with streetcars and sidewalks, streetlights and paved roads! And Timothy Eaton Mercantile Company's new store was said to be ten stories high! We knew Eaton's well from its huge catalog, which served as reading material and toilet paper in thousands of Canadian privies. The carefully examined ladies' underwear advertisements gave us our first little erections.

In Winnipeg the recent massive flu epidemic had occasioned strict sanitary regulations. When I told Grandmother Carter that it would cost her $25 to spit in the streets of Winnipeg, she told me in her emphatic tone, "I have no intention whatever of spitting in the streets of any city."

The massive manse at 572 Maryland Street in Winnipeg was a delight, for it had running hot and cold water and the first flush toilet we had ever seen, plus electric lights and an electric stove with a timing device that enabled my mother to let the Sunday roast and potatoes cook while we were in church. She always said that "the angels cooked the dinner."

The first excursion my brother and I made was to walk up Main Street to examine Eaton's new store. The rumors were true. It really was ten full stories high! We counted and recounted to make sure. We also tested thoroughly Eaton's moving staircases and elevators. And we saw people riding in streetcars and noted that automobiles went down the streets of Winnipeg leaving no dust in their wake. No dust at all!

Grandmother Carter approved of Winnipeg, and my Father went up in her estimation.

The Dodd family, our good friends from Rock Lake, arrived for a visit. Harry had come in part to show off his brand-new 1928 Pontiac sedan with its fixed roof, plush seats, and windows that rolled up and down. This automobile completely justified its claim of being "Chief of the Sixes." Harry took my father, my brother, and me for a spin going west out of the city along Portage la Prairie Avenue. My brother and I, sitting in the back seat, heard my father lean over to whisper to the proud driver, "Ease her up to forty, Harry, just to show the lads what it's like." Harry replied with a condescending smile, "You know, Gawge, this thing can go forty miles an hour all day long! *All day long!*"

I remember thinking, "Wow!"

Shortly after this outing, my father turned in the Model T for a slightly used 1928 Chevrolet, which he drove with an exuberance unmatched by skill. Since the six members of our family taxed the internal dimensions of the car, Father had my brother and me lie between the motor and the front fenders, hanging on to the headlights' bar, often for dear life, as we swung around corners.

Dad became an enthusiastic tennis player on the court next door but one from our house. I often served as ball boy and lighter of the fire in the gas heater that warmed water for Father's bath. During the final set he would say, "Bobbie, slide downstairs" — I was always told to *slide* on all my missions — "and fight the lire." I would reply, "Fes, Yather." With Father, we talked in spoonerisms.

One year a major tennis tournament — possibly the Canadian Open — was held at the Winnipeg Canoe and Racket Club. As a reward for my ball-boying, and knowing my interest in tennis, my father invited me to go with him. I was thrilled and proud to be going to such an important event with my handsome, well-dressed father. Then, for some reason, Dad said he was sorry but he would not be able to take me. I was heartbroken. I remember going to my father and telling him directly that I thought it was not right for him to tell me I could go and then tell me I couldn't. I shall always remember his reply:

"Bobbie, you are right. I made a mistake. Of course we'll go together."
We went first to Eaton's, where I was fitted with a gray-flannel Eton suit.
It was one of the proudest and happiest days of my life — and one of
the many reasons I respected and loved my father.

Dad played chess with great enthusiasm. Like his sermons, his game
was innovative and unorthodox. He constantly experimented with wacky
openings and surprising gambits without really knowing what he was
doing. He loved to tell about the time at the Canoe Club he was playing
with a distinguished player — he might even have been a Grand Master
— who knew all the standard openings. He certainly had never seen anything like the wild opening my father offered him. He studied it carefully
and responded cautiously. My father then made some crazy move.

The champion was taken aback. He analyzed the board for some
time, and finally said, "Brilliant! Absolutely brilliant! I believe you have
me, Reverend! I resign."

Dad had the presence of mind to say calmly, "Thank you. I enjoyed
the game."

My father's smoking posed problems because the congregation did
not approve. He therefore worked out a plan for dealing with visitors,
a scheme that involved the whole family. Each of us was given an
assignment. At the first sign of a church member approaching the front
door, Father gave the signal, "Parishioner at the gate!" and his troops
sprang into action. I collected ashtrays, my brother opened windows,
one sister fanned the air with a newspaper, while another lit incense
and walked slowly through the downstairs rooms. My mother, after a
long pause to allow for fumigation, opened the door and graciously
welcomed the visitor.

My father's method of smoking was peculiar. He never inhaled, and
on the rare occasions when he took smoke into his mouth, he would
immediately blow it out in a cloud. The cigarette would simply burn in
his mouth, gathering ash until it was long enough to drop onto his vest.
One day I asked him why he smoked at all — he might just as well set
the cigarette on a shelf and let it burn there. He replied, "I know, lad,
but the smoke curls up my nose and makes me a bit dizzy."

To this day I regret one of my comments. Because Dad felt guilty about the money he spent on tobacco, he bought a cheap and particularly foul-smelling weed called Wings. They were king-size and cost a quarter for two packs. He would economize by smoking them half down, butting them, and saving the butt behind his right ear. One Sunday morning at the close of the service, I met him at the church door and said, "You know, Dad, you have half a cigarette behind your ear." His look of sheer anguish made me wish with all my heart that I could call back those words.

I was educated at the John M. King Elementary School in Winnipeg over whose door was sunk deep in foot-high letters, KNOWLEDGE IS POWER. It was there I learned that arithmetic was some mysterious and frightening thing that I would never understand. I was led to this realization by a forbidding spinster of dreadful eye and bass voice named Miss Brown, who wore flowered, short-sleeved dresses and never shaved under her arms. This I discovered when she drilled us on multiplication. She would line up ten pupils in front of the room, go down the line and, standing before each victim, raise her right arm and, lowering it with energetic fervor, bellow a question. My question was *"Six times seven?"* and it threw me into a panic. I had mastered six times six but had no idea whether I should add another six or a seven to that number. I trembled, speechless before her. Miss Brown thundered her question anew, then again and again. After a long and dreadful silence, she ordered me to sit down.

When I was nine, I joined a secret society. We had three members and we called ourselves the White Stars, named after a white peppermint with a star imprinted on its side. Initiation rites consisted of swallowing three whole mints in rapid succession. Our secret sign — which I am about to divulge for the first time — was written in indelible ink on the palm of our left hand: *MmC*, with the smaller *m* inside the larger one and both letters placed within the curve of the *C*. The letters, in the language we had invented, stood for *Meni medi Corochi*, magic words that stood for "Death Before Dishonor." We flashed our palms at one another as a sign of recognition. Our society was dedicated to "Brave

Deeds of Chivalry" and "Secret Message Deliveries," for which purpose we built rapid deployment machines. They were constructed from two roller skates mounted in line on a one-by-six board on which I had bolted a soap box with wooden handlebars. My scooter was named Shooting Star. I don't recall performing a single brave deed of chivalry, but I delivered dozens of secret messages at breakneck speed.

A shining moment in our family's life came in 1927 during the visit of His Royal Highness, David, Prince of Wales, to Winnipeg on the occasion of the Diamond Anniversary of the Dominion. Mother was invited to the tea given in his honor and asked to give a speech welcoming him — "the world's most eligible bachelor" — on behalf of the women of Winnipeg. She bought a new dress, hat, and gloves, and looked smashing. The speech was a grand success; we were all very proud of her.

American School Days

Soon after Mother's starring role, my father was "called" to be minister of a large Congregational church in Minneapolis. Great excitement as we all went to get passports and new clothing for our new lives in the States. This was going to be an exciting adventure. Like all Canadians, we had feelings of both envy and resentment about the U.S. We saw it as a country of power and glamor, but we resented our sense that we could not measure up to Americans.

My first day in the Margaret Fuller School was not auspicious. The fifth-grade class was studying the geography of Manitoba and the teacher, after graciously introducing me as "a real live Canadian" who would know how to spell Winnipeg, gave me the privilege of writing it on the board for the class. I misspelled it.

We had arrived in Minneapolis in September 1929, just in time for the Wall Street crash. During one week in October, seven of my father's parishioners committed suicide. I never did know why, but I know that Dad never felt comfortable in this church and in 1932 he was asked to leave. I now think that his refusal to respect conventional attitudes toward what is often called sin, his informal style of preaching (that included dramatic readings from Tennyson and other poets), his penchant for "comforting the afflicted and afflicting the comfortable," and his insistence that the Gospel of Jesus Christ has social relevance, must have discomfited his conservative board of deacons.

I spent my adolescent years in Benson, a farming community in western Minnesota where my father was pastor of the Congregational church. While we lived in Benson, Mother contracted throat cancer. During my junior year in high school, she underwent a number of brutal operations that left her bedridden without a larynx and incapable of speech.

I was active in "declamation" and represented our high school in out-of-town contests. Mother, who was always interested in elocution, listened to me rehearse speeches and wrote critical notes I found immensely helpful. She also wanted to hear my father's sermons, so he asked a parishioner to run a telephone line between his pulpit and Mother's bed. She listened to his sermons and criticized them as she had done throughout their married life. When he came home from church, he would kiss her and she would hand him several pages of critical notes, which he always took in good heart.

Mother's funeral is still fresh in my mind. Instead of preaching a conventional funeral sermon, Father presented a beautifully crafted, lighthearted, and gracious tribute to the woman he loved.

I also remember the tribute paid by an old family friend, the Reverend John Johns. When he was a young man, his fine tenor voice had been heard in the Welsh National Men's Chorus. He sang a cappella, first in English, then in Welsh, one of Mother's favorite hymns to the hauntingly beautiful tune of "Aberystwyth," Mother's alma mater:

Jesu, lover of my soul, let me to Thy bosom fly
While the nearer waters roll, while the tempest still is high.
Hide me, O my Savior, hide, 'til the storms of life are past:
Safe into the haven guide, O receive my soul at last.

After my mother's dreadful illness and death, Father went through difficult years, finally resigned, and accepted a parish in the little village of Marietta, Minnesota, close to the even smaller hamlet of Revillo, South Dakota. Revillo is memorable for the slogan of its weekly hand-set newspaper. It is debatable whether the *Chicago Tribune* was really "The World's Greatest Newspaper" and one may doubt that the *New York Times* has always printed "All the News That's Fit to Print." But the

Revillo Times' slogan was unassailable. On the front page under its name appears its slogan in 24-point Cheltenham type: "The Only Newspaper in the World That Gives a Damn About Revillo, South Dakota."

My unmarried sister Stella kept house for Dad in Marietta, where he was happy and popular. Life there reminded him, I think, of his early years in Canadian villages. He had a large garden again, played chess and cribbage, wrote poetry, and enjoyed joking with the villagers. I remember coming home from college during the late 1930s and going to the little church to hear my father preach. After the service one Sunday, he met me at the door and said, "I don't know how that struck you, lad, but it bored me to tears."

My father later was hit by several minor strokes that left him partially paralyzed. But he kept on preaching, pulling himself slowly up to the pulpit by a rail he had constructed. One evening, while playing cribbage in the living room with the village drunkard, and grinning happily over a 24-count hand, he fell over dead. The church was filled to standing room for his funeral. He was buried in the plain pine coffin he had wanted.

We had trouble getting it for him. Since there was no "undertaker" — comforting euphemism, that — in Marietta, we were forced to negotiate with the smarmy salesman in Madison, Minnesota, a town some ten miles away. He tried to sell us an expensive casket "worthy" of my father. When I told him that no casket ever built was worthy of my father, that he had wanted a simple pine coffin, the salesman said, "Well, I'm sure your father's parishioners will be very disappointed, very disappointed indeed." I said that I doubted that, because they knew my father; at any rate, it was not their funeral, it was my father's, and by gum he was going to get what he had wanted.

During one of my last visits to Marietta, while I was in the Army, Dad had asked me about my citizenship. I told him I had taken out citizenship papers and asked him why he had never become an American citizen. He said the matter had troubled him for years but he had finally decided not to do so, because it would have obliged him to "break faith and foreswear allegiance" to all other countries. He could not bring himself to break faith and foreswear allegiance to his king and country. If he had been asked to *keep* faith and bear allegiance to all peoples, he would gladly have done so.

BENSON HIGH SCHOOL

Since there was no high school in Marietta, I decided to stay on alone and finish school in Benson, Minnesota. Those were memorable and happy years. My brother, Greg, who was working in a filling station, let me sleep in his rented room until I became houseboy, gardener, and chauffeur for a wealthy widow. I washed dishes for my food in Rangaard's Café — "Just Wonderful Food" — and I earned spending money by clerking Saturdays until 10 P.M. at the JC Penney store (his middle name really was Cash). The pay was only $2.50 a day, but during the worst of the depression, a dollar went a long way. Hamburgers, Cokes, coffee, candy bars, and a glass of beer cost five cents; movies were fifteen cents, gasoline twenty cents a gallon, eggs fifteen cents a dozen.

Benson was a heavily Norwegian community. I loved to listen to the lilt of Norwegian accents as families shared their week's experiences at *lutefisk* and *lefsa* suppers during Lutheran church socials, or as farmers enjoyed the pleasure of one another's company as they met on Main Street Saturday nights:

"Well, are yew in town tonight too, Sven?"

"Ya, I came in."

"Ya, I see that. . ."

"Well, I'll tall yew I had a time coming in from Six Mile Grove tonight! I was driving in nice as you please in my Model T car, and along comes Ole Swenson and he was going to pass me. Well, I wasn't going to let that happen, I can tell yew! Not as long as I'm around here!

No, siree! So I gave her the yuice and he gave her the yuice, and dar we stood, neck on neck, *tirty miles a hour!*"

One Saturday evening in the store, while I was selling a pair of Super Ox-Hide blue jeans (cost: $1.09) to a farmer, his young son came up to the counter, tugged gently on his father's worn old jeans and said, "Papa, please to give me one penny worth for yelly beans." The father looked down kindly at his son, pushed his huge, calloused hand into a pocket, brought out some change and said, "Here, little Ole, here are *three* cents for yelly beans. It's Saturday night! What the heck do we care for expenses?!" Ole skipped happily out of the store to share his wealth with friends.

I was the mad villain in our junior class play. The convoluted plot of *Murder in the Tower* has long been forgotten, but the ending never will be. After murdering an alarming number of victims, I had been cornered in a tower and was hiding in a packing case whose open end was turned toward the wings. I was supposed to shoot myself and had been armed for that purpose with the athletic department's starting pistol. The still-living members of the cast were waiting in the wings for the shot that was their cue to rush onto the stage and end the play.

Everything depended on that shot. But the pistol jammed and I could not get the darn thing to fire. Miss Arneson's frantic gestures from the wings were no help. I struggled with the pistol for an eternity of at least two minutes. It refused to fire. Finally, in desperation, I yelled, "BANG!" That produced a storm of good-hearted cheers from the audience.

I was the quarterback on the football team and seldom carried the ball. And that was just as well. As Coach Leon Brockmeyer said, I had a deceptive change of pace: First I ran slowly, then to cross up the opposition, I suddenly slowed down. He had me play "blocking back" in the now defunct single-wing formation made famous by Bernie Bierman's Golden Gophers of the University of Minnesota.

I don't recall seeing a more disgusted look on a human face than on "Brock's" when I told him how I had broken my toe and could not play in a big game on Saturday. The bedroom that I shared with Greg was down a long hall and around a corner from the bathroom. I played a game with myself, flushing the john, then tearing down the slippery hall to see if I could jump into bed before the flushing stopped. That fateful Friday night, I had slipped as I rounded the corner, slammed my toe against a door casing, and ended in a doctor's office. A year later I only partially redeemed myself in the coach's eyes by intercepting a badly thrown pass and staggering across the line for a winning touchdown.

In another football game, Pete Olson provided an unforgettable illustration of the rhetorical power of a single word to save a desperate situation. Benson High was about to start a game against Montevideo, a much larger and impressively equipped school. They had bleachers and bright lights for night games. Our school had no bleachers and we had never played under lights. Their team seemed enormous, and they were dressed in shiny purple uniforms with huge white numbers. The kid who was supposed to pack our game uniforms had forgotten them, so we had to play in torn and faded maroon sweatshirts. Our morale was already low when six pretty cheerleaders in smart uniforms led their fans in a chant that echoed through the valley: "Mon-te-vi-de-o! . . . Mon-te-vi-de-o! . . . Mon-te-vi-de-o!" We felt sunk, depressed, and totally demoralized.

We had no uniformed cheerleaders. We had only Pete Olson, sitting high in the bleachers, who had a badly cleft palate. But his soul was on fire, and he was not in the least impressed with the enemy's display of raw power. He knew exactly the appropriate word for the occasion. During the awed silence that followed the Montevideo massed cheer, his high-pitched voice rang out loud and clear: *"Oh, apple-thauth!"*

Transformed, we threw back our heads and laughed, yelled defiance, then took the field and won the game.

44

High School Reunion
and a Sixteen-Cent Tax

In high school, I forgot all about Birdy Bennett and fell in love with Karen, a lovely and lively Scandinavian girl who wore Tweed perfume. To this day, whenever I get a whiff of that perfume, I am transported back to dances in the Benson Armory or Glenwood Lakeside Pavilion and to the back seat of cars on long, happy, and romantic rides to basketball games in neighboring towns.

One day in 1987 — some thirty-five years after Anne and I were married — I received a letter postmarked Benson, Minnesota, from Mildred Torgeson. That name brought back a flood of memories. Mildred was the large and good-natured girl who was everybody's friend and the secretary of our class. She had sat one row in front of me and two seats to the left in Miss Arneson's World History class. It was great to hear from her again. She was inviting me to return for the fortieth anniversary of our graduation.

The class had made elaborate preparations. We would have a dinner dance at the new (since our time) Benson Golf Club. The dance was to be "formal," the dancing to "our kind of music." That meant "Deep Purple," "Red Sails in the Sunset," and "I Sailed Away to Treasure Island."

Anne agreed that it would be fun to go. Although she told me she would be darned if she'd ever wear Tweed perfume, she looked forward to seeing Karen, of whom she had heard so much. For the formal dance, Anne bought a handsome summer cocktail dress from the Women's Exchange in Williamstown, where she worked — a volunteer used-clothing store whose profits went to the Visiting Nurse Association. The dress had been an expensive polka dot with a narrow black belt.

The night before the big party and all the next day, as we drove the 140 miles from Anne's home in Minneapolis to western Minnesota, I kept thinking of what I would say to Karen and she to me. We had once meant a great deal to each other. What, I wondered, would she say to me? What would be the first tender words we would share after all those years? Did any sparks linger in the coals of adolescent passion?

When we unpacked our suitcase in Benson's only motel — the old Paris Hotel on Main Street having burned down — Anne discovered that she had forgotten to pack the black belt indispensable to her costume. I told her not to worry. I, who had worked at JC Penney, could surely find her a belt. We looked in Penney's and a women's dress shop. No suitable belts. Then I saw a new shop. We entered and Anne explained her problem to the rather heavy, pleasant woman of late middle age behind the cash register. She said she had no belts but something that might do. She suggested a length of black-velvet roping that Anne might tie about her like a monk's belt. A good idea. We bought about a yard and a half and the following conversation ensued:

> *She:* I don't know whether to charge sales tax for ornamentation or no tax for wearing apparel. If you're not from Minnesota, you may not understand about the problem of sales taxes.
>
> *I:* Oh, we understand. We're from Massachusetts; we have sales taxes.
>
> *She:* Massachusetts? Then you must be Bob Waite. I'm Karen. [Then, glancing at Anne] You owe me sixteen cents for the tax.

My Flirtation with Disaster

My high school years in Benson, Minnesota, had been happy ones. But I came within an ace of ruining my life — let alone an academic career — by one act of monumental adolescent folly. If I had been charged with manslaughter, I would have pleaded guilty.

A group of us teenagers were celebrating our graduation from high school in 1937 with a dinner at a friend's summer cottage on Lake Minnewaska before going to a gala dance at the Lakeside Pavilion in Glenwood, Minnesota. After the meal, while waiting to go to the dance, we were sitting around the spacious, rustic living room, reminiscing about our happy school years. Hanging on the wall behind me was a high-powered hunting rifle with telescopic sights.

I took it down and began drawing a bead on my closest friends. "Karen," I said, "I've got you right between the eyes . . . Kay, I've got you right over the heart . . . Mike, it's your turn next . . ." and so on around the room. To show off, I had planned to pull the trigger, just to hear it click. I fully intended to. Indeed, I still remember the feel of my finger as it tightened on the cool, curved metal. Then, suddenly, inexplicably, the barrel swung six inches to the left as I finished pulling the trigger. It did not click. It blasted a four-inch hole through the front door.

I still live with the memory of that ghastly moment. It was as if someone had clubbed me on the chest with a two-by-four. I was physically sick with feelings of shock and shame at the totality of my stupidity. I knew that I had very nearly killed one of my dearest friends and ruined my own life.

I also knew that I had been saved only by the grace of God. That terrible experience mightily buttressed my religious faith.

Macalester College and Sleeping with John Wilkes Booth

A number of summer jobs helped finance my undergraduate years at Macalester College in St. Paul. I stripped bluegrass — a process not generally known outside grass country — in the hayfields of Minnesota. The seed, I was told, was then shipped to Kentucky, cleaned, and packaged as "Kentucky Bluegrass." I poured concrete for grain elevators in South Dakota. I shoveled ore in the open-pit iron mines on the Mesabi Range. And I was paid to sleep with the corpse of John Wilkes Booth, the man who shot Lincoln.

That happened in this wise: I had heard that the Arturis Mine near Bovey, Minnesota, was hiring workers at the then generous rate of 37½ cents an hour. I hitchhiked to Bovey to learn that I could have a job but that the Arturis would start hiring in a week. Since I was down to my last two dollars and I wanted to eat and needed a place to sleep, I joined one of the concessions attached to the Bazinette Shows, a small carnival that had stopped in town.

Mr. and Mrs. Brewster were an elderly Southern couple who had rented space in the carnival to display a body that was their source of livelihood. Clad in a pair of worn Boy Scout shorts, the cadaver lay on a table under a home-built wooden canopy mounted on the platform of a ton-and-a-half International truck bearing South Carolina license plates. At the rear of the truck was a small ticket booth where Mr. Brewster collected the entrance fee of fifteen cents a look. Removable stairs allowed customers to enter one side of the display, walk around the table, and exit on the other side. What they would see, the Brewsters were convinced, was the actual body of Lincoln's assassin.

According to Mrs. Brewster, John Wilkes Booth had not died in Garrett's burning barn on the night of 26 April 1865. He had been rescued by Southern sympathizers who viewed him as a hero for killing the "tyrannical" President who had ruined the South. For some twenty years, Booth had appeared in stage dramas in the deep South. But he took to heavy drinking and, in a fit of depression, swallowed a massive dose of arsenic, which, along with the alcohol and formaldehyde, preserved his body for posterity. Mrs. Brewster had inherited the corpse from her paternal grandfather and had exhibited it successfully in Southern states. But when interest languished, she decided to bring him north to see how he would play to audiences in Iowa and Minnesota.

The Brewsters had collected a great deal of memorabilia that was displayed in locked glass-covered cases: posters, bills, and enthusiastic reviews of his many plays (including *Hamlet, Romeo and Juliet, Julius Caesar*), a signet ring with the initials JWB, linen handkerchiefs with the same letters, an x-ray of Booth's leg showing the tibia fractured two inches above the left ankle, broken the night of 14 April in Ford's Theater, Washington, D.C. (In jumping down from Lincoln's box to the stage, it will be recalled, Booth had caught a spur in the flag that draped the presidential box.) The Brewster collection also showed x-rays of the cadaver's teeth and a poster offering $5,000 to anyone who could prove that this was *not* the body of John Wilkes Booth. We had no takers.

My job was to guard this valuable property and preserve it from further deterioration. At night I slept beside the cadaver's table, still redolent of formaldehyde, on a removable canvas Army cot. I was provided with two smelly Army blankets and a ten-pound jar of Vaseline with which to rub "all of him down every night before going to bed." Mr. Brewster added pointedly, "And I mean all of him."

Skeptics may doubt that I rubbed down the actual body of John Wilkes Booth, but I can assure them that every night for a week I did massage the cadaver of a nineteenth-century uncircumcised male.

When the Arturis Mine opened the following Monday, my hands were the softest and most pliable among the shovelers of ore.

Rubbing down John Wilkes Booth

KENNETH HOLMES AND
EARNING OUR HERITAGE

My first year at Macalester College was an awakening intellectual experience that persuaded me that there was something to the old definition of a college professor as someone who liked college life and decided not to leave it.

I owe a lifelong debt of gratitude to Professor Kenneth L. Holmes for serving as my first role model. He introduced me to the Lady Clio, muse of history, and instructed me in techniques that might be used in wooing that elusive lady. His sprightly lectures brought historical personalities and events alive; his trenchant criticisms of many papers gave me a thorough grounding in methods of historical research. He and his wife, Martha, of engaging humor, delightful lisp, and soft Kentucky drawl, often invited students to their comfortable home on Summit Avenue, where we had great fun at informal dinner parties that made me want to emulate their lifestyle.

The most valuable single course I have ever taken was at Macalester. It was called English 1, but it was actually a rich and carefully designed introduction to the humanities, based on a huge two-volume work edited by two Macalester professors, Frank Ward and Grace May, and cogently titled *Earning Our Heritage*. The title was inspired by Goethe's comment *"Was du ererbt von deinen Väter hast / Erwirb es um es zu besitzen"* (What you have inherited from your fathers, you must earn in order to possess).

The course was tough and rewarding. During the year we read, discussed, and wrote essays on such works as a novel and a poem by

Thomas Hardy; John Milton's *Il Penseroso,* the Book of Job, Aristophanes' *The Frogs,* Shakespeare's *The Tempest,* James Joyce's *Portrait of an Artist as a Young Man,* Goethe's *Faust,* and A. S. Eddington's *The Nature of the Physical World.*

I recall writing an essay on *The Aeneid* with the ambitious title "The Epic Tradition," for which my father composed an equally ambitious sonnet that served as an introduction, "On Reading Virgil for the First Time."

I found the course humbling, for I discovered in a hurry how much there was for me to learn.

One of my friends at Macalester College was a refugee from Czechoslovakia. František Kreysa had sailed in 1939 on the German liner *Bremen,* which, after the outbreak of war, had been interned in New York. The Czech consulate in Minneapolis–St. Paul had arranged a scholarship for Kreysa at Macalester, and he lived down the hall from me. His German was better than his English. I, who was struggling with what Mark Twain called that "Awful German Language," helped him with his English and he reciprocated by conversing with me in German.

We both enjoyed skating on the outdoor college rink. One fine winter's evening the rink was graced by a smashing young blonde dressed in abbreviated costume, who was skating magnificently. Frank and I were commenting in German about her physical charms and what it would be like to spend a night with her. He interrupted me to say that if we were going to talk like *that* he had better say it in Czech, which he proceeded to do. Whereupon the lovely young lady whirled around and slapped him across the face. Hard. She also spouted a torrent of unintelligible deprecations.

I skated up to Frank and asked him what that was all about. He was in a state of shock. "My God," he finally gasped, "this is terrible! Terrible! Do you know who that was? That was Vera Hruba, the Czech Olympic champion!"

Norman Elliott, one of my closest friends in college — and ever since — stuttered very badly when he was in college. Both of us served as undergraduate advisors to freshmen. We arrived on campus a few days early in the autumn to welcome the incoming class and to help them through their first days at Macalester. We were standing on the campus one afternoon when a gigantic future defensive tackle at least six feet seven, weighing some 280 pounds and wearing, incongruously, a little green freshman "beanie," approached Elliott and stuttered, "Can you p-p-p-please t-t-t-t-tell me w-where the d-d-d-d-dean's office is?" Elliott immediately turned on his heel and left the two of us standing there. I directed the freshman to the dean and then caught up with my friend. "Why the hell didn't you answer that freshman? We're supposed to be friendly and you just walked away from him!"

Elliott replied, "You th-th-think I w-w-w-want m-m-my d-d-d-d-damned head kn-kn-kn-kn-knocked off?"

A MILITARY INTERLUDE:
The Night I Saved Our Country

After graduating from Macalester in 1941, I was drafted into the Army of the United States. Mine could not be called a distinguished military career. I was inducted at Fort Snelling, Minnesota, "the oldest fort west of the Mississippi River." Since I had weak eyes and a deaf ear, nerve damage from a bout of scarlet fever at the age of nine, I was marked "Limited Service" and assigned to the induction station at the fort. I interviewed inductees to determine how their civilian skills might best fit military needs. For example, the Army manual told us that because of their sensitive ears, violin players made excellent mine sappers. I shudder to think of the number of fine violinists from the Minneapolis Symphony Orchestra I sent to Germany to be blown up.

I took my basic training at the Fort. Our drill sergeant was an intimidating professional soldier named Sergeant Fischer. Six feet six, he weighed 250 fat-free pounds, spoke in a heavy South Dakota German accent, and had a heart of pure iron. He also had an effective pedagogical technique. He would repeat his instructions with machine-gun rapidity, followed by a statement in the same tempo and a concluding expletive. Consider his description of the "long thrust" bayonet drill:

"Now soldiers in the bayonet drill we have the long trust the long trust the long trust any questions shutup gotdarnit." His description of sanitation was unique. "And now I vill instruct in military sanitation in military sanitation any questions shutup and you vill listen gotdarnit. I see you soldiers out in the field out in the field and you hear the call of nature the call of nature that means you feel you must defecate you must def-e-cate that is to say like you soldiers say you need to take a shit take a crap take a shit take a crap is that clear anyquestionsshutup. In the field there is no latrine gotdarnit no latrine no latrine at all so vat to do? You dig yourself a little hole a little hole a little hole gotdarnit then you take down your pants and you do it. But then you fail to cover up the hole! gotdarnit *you fail to cover up the hole!* and it is a vorm day it is a vorm day a very vorm day remember that gotdarnit.

"Now meantime the field kitchen has come up and the cook says to himself gotdarnit 'I vill make for these soldiers a nice evening meal a nice evening meal. I vill even make for them a lemon mirage pie a lemon mirage pie is that clear anyquestions shutup.' And he sets that pie out on a munitions case to cool to cool gotdarnit.

"All right. So now there comes a little fly buzzing around all around gotdarnit it is a nice vorm day a nice vorm day so he buzzes around then he sees your crap in the hole *because you failed to cover up that hole* got-darnit and he says to himself, 'Oho! Here is a nice juicy turd. A nice juicy turd.' So he lands and he I don't know what he does he plays around on that turd then he flies around some more and he says, 'Oho! Here is a nice lemon mirage pie that is my favorite pie gotdarnit.' So he lands on the pie!!"

"That soldiers is not is not is not military sanitation gotdarnit any questions shut up."

When my grandson asked me what I did in the great war, I told him about the night when it was twenty-nine degrees below zero with a thirty-mile-per-hour wind shooting snow horizontally across the Mendota Bridge, which stretches far across the Mississippi River between Minneapolis and St. Paul. I drew guard duty and was assigned to defend that bridge, surely the coldest and most desolate place in the state of Minnesota.

I put on all of my winter issue: two pairs of woolen underwear, woolen shirt, sweater, field jacket, overcoat, two pairs of woolen socks, boots and heavy buckled overshoes, woolen gloves, woolen mitts, and leather overmitts. My head swaddled in woolen cap and a heavy woolen muffler, I waddled about with the dexterity and speed of a ruptured hippopotamus. How I could have put a rifle to my shoulder, aimed it, and pulled the trigger with my mittened hand I could not imagine.

When I returned from my first tour of the bridge, bucking the great wind that drove the snow into my face and froze ice on my glasses, making "zero visibility" a reality, I asked the sergeant of the guard what I was supposed to be doing. It is not a question usually asked in the Army, but he answered it: "You, soldier, are guarding this important bridge from Japanese air attack."

I told my grandson with no little pride that I succeeded in that heroic task. For not one Japanese Zero dared bomb the Mendota Bridge while I was guarding it that night with a 1903 Springfield single-shot bolt-action rifle.

*"You, soldier, are guarding this important bridge
from Japanese air attack."*

Courtship and Marriage

The best thing that happened to me in the Army was that while stationed at Fort Snelling, I met Anne Barnett on a blind date. We recited favorite poems and she corrected my rendition of *Young Lochinvar*. We fell in love that night, the eve of Memorial Day, 1943. We were engaged on Bastille Day and married on Labor Day. Years later we both agreed that it had been too long a courtship.

Like many other wartime romances, ours had been intense and strikingly energetic. Whenever I could leave Fort Snelling, I went to Anne's home in southern Minneapolis just three blocks from Lake Harriet. We canoed across the lake and walked around it dozens of times while talking about everything from religion and ballet to literature and sports, from her experience with archery to her discontent with sorority life, which she found stuffy and snobbish. She had pledged largely to please her mother and her grandmother, who had been a member of the Alpha chapter of Kappa Kappa Gamma. We played tennis and swam. We ate popcorn as we listened to band concerts at the Lakeside Pavilion. We didn't talk much about music. I remember asking Anne if they had any serious music in her house. She said, "Well, yes, we have Danny Deaver." When I said that was not really serious, she said, "What do you mean, not serious? They hanged him didn't they?"

When Anne received her degree from the University of Minnesota that summer, I attended the graduation ceremonies. I wanted to get her a noteworthy present to mark the occasion. In an antique/junk shop in St. Paul I finally found what I wanted: an enormous, great, gray owl with a five-foot wingspread, solemn expression, and glassy eye. It cost a month's Army pay to purchase him and have him crated and trucked to Anne's home. I enclosed a message saying that his name was Lochinvar, that he was symbolic of her newly acquired wisdom and also of her sorority (I had not known that she had just resigned from the sorority when its president informed her coldly, "Kappas do not go into nursing. We disapprove.")

Lochinvar made a great hit with Anne's mother and father, but not with her stern and proper grandmother, who informed her that "gentlemen in my day gave ladies flowers, candy, or handkerchiefs but *never* stuffed owls." I am sure she was right about that.

My father, who struck it off beautifully with Anne, drove from Marietta to officiate at our wedding in Anne's home. I got a ten-day furlough from Fort Snelling, borrowed some light camping equipment, and we spent our honeymoon canoeing from northern Minnesota into Canada. It was mid-September and the weather was perfect: warm sunbright days, sparkling clear waters, cool nights, no bugs, no people, and glorious silence. Sheer magic. Returning to base camp on our little island one late afternoon at the end of the first week, I was paddling in the stern and Anne was lying bare-breasted and beautiful with her legs draped over the gunwales. We had passed under a cliff and bits of shale had dropped into the canoe. For half a lazy hour Anne had been picking up little pieces of shale, dropping each one gently into the lake, watching each piece form expanding circles in the still, dark water. Then another, then another. "You know," she said pensively, "this is the most fun I've had since we've been up here." I tipped her out of the canoe.

From Fort Snelling I was shipped to the induction center at Jefferson Barracks, Missouri, where we processed draftees from the Ozarks, among other places. I particularly remember Wilbur, for he gave me a memorable demonstration of how words can change their meaning.

Wilbur was a charming Li'l Abner from the hills of western Kentucky. He had not learned to read or write and he didn't talk much. He was deeply religious and lonely and he liked to tell me about his family at home. He was particularly close to his widowed mother. She meant, he said, "'bout everythin'" to him. Just before he was to be shipped overseas, he came to me and said he had heard that I could read and write real good, and asked if I would do him a big favor. I assured him I would be glad to. He said, "It's for my mother. I wonder if you'd write a letter for me to my dear old fuckin' mother."

One of the best soldiers in our outfit had the unfortunate name of Parts. Although he richly deserved a promotion, the sergeant major never put him up for corporal. He took too much delight in reading off the roster, "Parts! Pa-arts! Private Parts!"

Anne joined me when I was stationed in Jefferson Barracks. We lived in a dingy apartment in St. Louis and she got a job nursing in the Barnes Children's Hospital, where she fell in love with Charlie, an entrancing, abandoned five-year-old black kid who was dying of leukemia. He had become incontinent and he often called for Anne. When she arrived, he would hang his head in shame and say through his tears, "Noyce! Noyce! I done a *bad thing*, a *bad thing!*"

Anne's heart was broken when Charlie died in her arms. His words of remorse lived on in our family. Whenever I forgot to do something I had promised to do, or otherwise ticked Anne off, all I needed to say was "Noyce, I done a *bad thing!*" and she forgave me. I was careful to use this magic formula only on rare occasions.

PEANUT BUTTER
AT HARVARD GRADUATE SCHOOL

In the autumn of 1945, with the indispensable help of the GI Bill, I enrolled in Harvard University's graduate school to study for a doctorate in history.

In Cambridge Anne and I found an "efficiency apartment" in Felton Hall, a remarkable *ménage* that made up in atmosphere what it lacked in efficiency. A Swedish opera star had built it in the mid–nineteenth century as a dwelling place for young Harvard gentlemen who stabled their horses in the dirt-floored basement. Since it was fortuitously located just beyond the "prayer line," it was popular in its day. That line marked the boundary beyond which one could not hear the bell summoning undergraduates to eight-o'clock morning prayers at the chapel in the Yard.

The enormous current proprietor, a Mrs. Bartlett, let it be known that hers was a very special lineage. When I asked her if she were a member of the Daughters of the American Revolution, she replied, "Oh, dear, no! Much better than that!" She expanded herself to her full girth and concluded grandly, "I am a Mayflower girl." When I remarked, I hope dryly, that the Mayflower must have been an enormous ship, she replied, "Oh, dear, no, just a tiny little vessel! It brought only a few of us over. Just a few."

Felton Hall must have had the most distinguished janitor in metropolitan Boston. Mr. Berger, who had a flowing white mane and well-trimmed Vandyke, invariably wore a vested blue serge suit, white shirt, large bow tie, and pince-nez attached to a black ribbon. He read

Desiderius Erasmus and Sebastian Brandt, Dickens and Trollope, and recited with gusto a large repertoire of ribald limericks.

Our flat consisted of a large living-dining room with fourteen-foot ceilings and windows with heavy maroon tasseled drapes and one small bedroom. We also had a windowless bathroom and a waterless "efficiency kitchen," a former closet now equipped with a single hot plate and an electric oven, whose liner we used as a dishpan to wash the dishes that we carried to the bathroom. A folding shelf dropped down to cover the bathtub and form a table on which we did the dishes while sitting on the john.

Before I began to earn a small salary as a teaching fellow in history at Harvard College and Anne got a job shelving books in the Widener Library, we lived on the GI Bill, which paid us $110 a month. Fifty-five dollars went for rent (fifty for actual rent, five for ice we put into the ice-box that drained into the dirt cellar through a hole bored in the floor). That left $55 for food, clothing, beer, a very occasional movie, and any priceless frivolity we set our hearts on. Anne found a way to make a tin of Spam stretch for three meals. Christmas dinner was shared with fellow graduate students. One couple contributed a chicken, one the vegetables, one a bottle of bad wine and a store-bought pie. The first Christmas we exchanged presents costing a maximum of $1.50 each. I gave Anne the color lipstick she wanted, she gave me something I had never owned before: a bow tie from the Coop. I spent a good deal of Christmas morning with Mr. Berger standing behind me with his arms around my neck, teaching me how to tie it.

In those days, I smoked a pipe too heavily. Without telling Anne, I ordered five pounds of my favorite tobacco from a St. Paul tobacconist. It came C.O.D. and cost enough to wipe out a week's budget for food. I came home from a hard day at Widener Library to find on my supper plate a large serving of tobacco and a peanut-butter sandwich.

Someone in the University wanted to know how much it cost to raise a child from zero to three years of age. He hit on the happy idea of using the children of graduate students to find out. That meant that Geoffrey, born in 1946, got free orange juice and a free education at the nursery school, to which I wheeled him every day before going to the library. At the age of three when he graduated, he was given a splendid diploma complete with the Harvard *Veritas* seal in crimson emblazoned on heavy rag paper, with his name beautifully calligraphed along with the announcement that he was duly graduated from the Harvard Nursery School.

Shortly after his graduation, I had taken Geoffrey to the Yard, which he often used as a playground by crawling up and down the Widener steps. That day workmen were preparing the Tercentenary Theater for the university commencement ceremonies that would take place the following week. We met a distinguished older gentleman from the class of about '21 who asked Geoffrey jovially if he were planning to go to Harvard one day. To the surprise of the old alumnus, Geoff replied disdainfully, "I've *been* to Harvard." We had no way of knowing then that he would enter the Harvard class of 1969 and be graduated magna cum laude.

Every university has its share of aging eccentrics who manage to stay on long after graduation. Felton Hall had its full quota, and they enriched our lives. During our first week there, I had gone across the street to buy peanut butter at a small grocery store. The clerk asked me if I wanted it plain or homogenized. I had been accustomed to stirring the peanut oil into the mass of mashed peanuts, and I thought it would be fun to try the newfangled homogenized variety, even if it cost four cents more. So I said, "Homogenized, please." Whereupon I was turned around by a tousled-haired, tweedy man of fanatical eye. With both hands shaking me by my lapels, he looked me furiously in the eye and, his voice shaking with passion, sputtered, *"What did I hear you say?"* I repeated that I had ordered homogenized peanut butter. This response sent the man into a spasm of indignation: *"Hier ist der Untergang des Abendlandes!* Anybody, *anybody* who would eat homogenized peanut butter would, would drink a Coca-Cola!"

Having made that pronouncement, he slammed out of the store. Such was my introduction to Dr. Roberts, a sporadically employed philosopher who lived above us on the second floor.

*Anybody, **anybody** who would eat homogenized peanut butter would, would drink a Coca-Cola!"*

Miss Caflin was an ancient, wraithlike Sanskrit scholar who, since the turn of the century, had lived in her flat directly across from Dr. Roberts. She solved the problem of what to do with the heavy maroon brocaded window draperies. She wore them like togas. Black cotton stockings and high white Keds basketball shoes completed her ensemble. Since she knew perfectly well that electricity was only a passing fad, she refused to have it in her rooms. She did her translations of Sanskrit by flickering gaslight and wrote with a quill pen. A nephew in Concord supplied her with goose feathers.

Two bachelors lived next to each other on the third floor and shared a toilet. Mr. Hemple was a nearsighted, slightly paranoid German who suffered from hemorrhoids. One evening, when Anne was alone in our apartment, she heard the metal flap on the letter slot of our door open. She stooped to look through the slit and met Herr Hemple directly, eye to eye. He said, "I am yust looking to see if you haf your own WC. I haf to chare mine vit that crazy Voodmansey."

Mr. Woodmansey was not really crazy, he was only eccentric. An inventor, he kept trying to make ice without electricity. His *Lebenszweck*, however, was to create a new primary color, using grocery-store clothing dyes. That quest absorbed his waking hours, producing much friction with Herr Hemple and a major crisis in Felton Hall.

One warm June evening about midnight, we were awakened by screaming sirens and powerful lights shining through our ground-floor windows. A policeman shouted through our open window, "It's all right, lady, don't worry, we've got the place surrounded."

Later we learned that Hemple had gone to the toilet, and after a difficult bowel movement, observed the blood-red rags Woodmansey was dyeing in the toilet in the hope of discovering his new primary color. Convinced that he was hemorrhaging badly, Mr. Hemple, in a panic, had called both the Cambridge police and fire departments.

One Saturday evening a group of us graduate students sat in our living room eating popcorn and drinking our weekly one-quart ration of beer, meted out in small jelly glasses. The conversation turned to stories about our absent-minded professors. A fellow inmate of Felton Hall who was a graduate student at MIT told a charming story about Professor Norbert Wiener, the brilliant classicist-linguist-philosopher-mathematical physicist who was the father of cybernetics.

Wiener, a short, gnomelike man who was massively brachycephalic, wore Coke-bottle-bottomed glasses for myopia and was notoriously absent-minded. He lived in Cambridge. Every evening he took the subway home from MIT, got off at Harvard Square, and walked slowly up Boylston Avenue to his home. But one evening he had a problem. He remembered that the family had recently moved but he had forgotten the location of his new house. He saw a little girl skipping rope and asked her if she knew where the Wieners lived. "Yes," she said brightly, "they used to live in that white house over there, but they moved to that big brown house across the street near the corner." Wiener was grateful. "Thank you, little girl, you are a very smart little girl. Thank you very much!"

She replied, "Oh, you're welcome, Daddy."

History 1 and "One Dead Dawg"

I found teaching for three years in History 1 at Harvard College immensely valuable. The old-fashioned, demanding, year-long introductory course in European history helped bring together the narrative of that complex story. It was a good framework for the Ph.D. "orals" as well as for my own future career as a Europeanist.

During the first term we "covered" the story from the Merovingians and Charlemagne through feudalism to Innocent III to Luther and Henry VIII to the Renaissance and the French Revolution. During the second term we started with Napoleon, Metternich, Castlereagh, and vom Stein and went through Bismarck, Cavour, and Alexander II to Lloyd George, Lenin, and Hitler. ("It's a good course, but don't drop your pencil or you'll miss the Reformation.")

We teaching fellows led two discussion groups of some eighteen to twenty freshmen twice a week, after a senior member of the history department gave the weekly lecture and met with us to plan strategy for our discussion classes. In my day, the man in charge of the first term was Professor Charles Taylor, whose specialty was French feudalism. He was enormously conscientious about his lectures to freshmen. I remember seeing him pacing the corridor of New Lecture Hall each week chain-smoking cigarettes and muttering to himself before lecturing to some 200 freshmen.

Professor Michael Karpovich was in charge of the second semester. He was the esteemed mentor of Nicholas Riasonovsky, Martin Malia, Richard Pipes, and others who would become distinguished Russianists.

One of them — I think Pipes — told me that years later Karpovich had invited his seminar to spend a weekend with him at his huge dacha in Vermont that had a tree left growing through the living-room roof. The Soviets had just sent "mutnic" into space. She was named Laika, a bitch of no particular breed, who lived for seven days, proving that animals (and presumably humans) can live in space. It was shortly after this event that Karpovich and his guests were riding the very Russian emotional roller coaster from elation to dark despair. As the night wore on and the tea in the samovar grew bitter and cold, Karpovich became more and more morose. He shook his head and muttered despairingly, "Look at the world! Look at it! *Surrounded.* Surrounded by one dead dawg!"

I was also privileged to take one of the last classes Professor Howard McIlwain taught in medieval political theory, and to hear Professor George La Piana's last lectures on the Italian *risorgimento.*

WILLIAMSTOWN AND WILLIAMS COLLEGE

In spite of my unpromising "one beer" interview, I was hired by Williams College, where I taught for forty happy years.

We all loved the town. After about seven years, I had an opportunity to move to a large university. We held a family conference about the decision. Geoffry, our ten-year-old, said that he and Peter, his kid brother, had talked it over. They wanted me to be happy and to take the job I liked but asked me to promise them one thing: Don't move out of Williamstown. Except for research trips and visiting appointments, I never did.

We lived in a happy house on Talcott Road, just north of the town library, then located in the old Botsford House on the village green. There were a lot of kids in our neighborhood. In a small town, we have special celebrations for such events as Halloween. I particularly remember two such experiences.

One evening the leader of a group of sheet-wearing ghosts and goblins rang the bell at our front door. I was confronted by a seven-year-old ghost who held out an open pillowcase, smiled, and said, "Trick or treat!" I said that I'd like a trick, please.

She was confused by that response and asked me what I meant. I said that I thought I had been offered a choice, that "trickortreat" was more than one word that meant candy, it meant that if I didn't give a treat, a trick would be played on me. She had never heard of that interpretation but thought it might be fun. After consulting with her ghostly colleagues for a few minutes, she said, "All right, we'll play a trick on you. Our trick is a riddle. If you can answer our riddle, you don't have to give us a treat. But if you can't, you must give us twice as many treats."

Thinking that the little girl would get ahead in life, I agreed. She asked her riddle: "What is *big,* green, and yellow and hangs down from a tree?" I thought hard and fast as a half-dozen bright eyes behind black masks peered at me anxiously. Under great pressure, I folded and said, "Little girl, I do not know what is large, green, and yellow and hangs down from a tree." A beatific smile spread over her face and she said with triumphant joy, *"A dead Girl Scout!"*

A couple of years later we were confronted by a band of ghosts and ferocious little animal-like creatures. I looked with mock horror at one of them and said, "My goodness, you frighten me! What in the world are you?"

He said reassuringly, "Don't be scared, mister, I'm just a little boy who got dressed up for Halloween."

● ● ● ● ●

Shortly after arrival at Williams, I was asked to serve on the Faculty-Student Lecture Committee, charged with encouraging undergraduates to become actively involved in the process of inviting scholars, musicians, and other artists to the campus. We were delighted when Erwin Panofsky, the great art historian, accepted. He lectured on a Monday evening at 7:30. Mr. Panofsky was a shortsighted little man who hunched over the podium and, with his eyes about seven inches away, read his lecture. The delivery was not impressive, but the contents were superb. The audience was spellbound.

The following day, I lectured at 1:30 in the same hall to about 200 students from all sections of the introductory European history course. Shortly after my performance, I met a student in the men's toilet whom I recognized as a member of the lecture committee. I had seen him at Panofsky's splendid lecture the night before, but I had not known that he had just come from *my* lecture.

Thinking of the student's presence at the Panofsky lecture of the previous night, and wanting to know how a freshman had reacted to it, I asked what he thought of the lecture. He, thinking of my lecture that he had just left, seemed rather surprised that I should ask such a question. He said, "I don't know, sir, I guess it was OK." Furious that Panofsky's fine lecture should receive such indifferent reception, I exclaimed, "Just what do you mean, it was only OK? That lecture was brilliant! Indeed, that was the finest lecture given at Williams College since I came here . . . That, son, was a veritable *tour de force!*" Leaving the bewildered young man wide-eyed and speechless, I slammed out of the room.

Late that night I realized what I had done, and I could well imagine what the young man was thinking: "Good Lord, what an ego!" I spent the next three years waiting for that kid to graduate and leave town.

To introduce our students to the problems of historical interpretation, we gave young men — no women in those benighted days — in the freshman course conflicting contemporary sources dealing with famous historical events: for example, the conflict between secular and clerical accounts of the epic struggle between Henry IV, a medieval German king, and Hildebrand, the powerful Pope Gregory VII, as it reached its dramatic climax before the walls of the papal castle at Canossa in the Italian Alps. The Pope had excommunicated the king, and it was obvious to Henry that he could never be elected Holy Roman Emperor of the German Nation if he did not first receive absolution and support from Pope Gregory. Henry made the long, painful journey in the dead of winter to the Pope's castle. A monastic writer recorded the event in famous lines: "There, before the castle walls at Canossa stood the proud Henry, in abject surrender, lamenting in sackcloth and ashes, baring his breast and standing barefoot in the snow for three days and three nights."

After reading this and several conflicting accounts, students were required to write a five-page essay entitled "What Really Happened at Canossa in January 1077." One freshman was caught up in the drama:

We must put ourselves back into one of the most dramatic scenes of all history: There, secure and comfortable in his impregnable castle, sits the great medieval Pope Gregory VII. Here approaches the once proud and haughty King Henry IV, now an abject penitant in sackcloth covered with ashes. More than that: In the bitter cold and wind of winter, he stands barefoot in the snow for three days and three nights abusing himself in front of the Pope. Is it not an unbelievable *scene?* [Student's emphasis]

In the margin of the paper I wrote, "Unbelievable is certainly the *mot juste.*"

ALEKSANDR FURSENKO AT WILLIAMS

In October 1968 Williams College entertained the first Soviet historian who had been authorized to leave the USSR on a private research trip. Aleksandr Vasilevich Fursenko, a member of the Institute of History in Leningrad, lectured on American history at the institute and had written a study of the Rockefeller oil interests. He was in the States to study the American electoral campaign of 1968 and was particularly interested in Nelson Rockefeller's bid for the presidency. He had come to Williamstown to interview James MacGregor Burns, whose biography of Franklin Roosevelt he greatly admired. Jim had invited him to speak at the college; he had accepted and prepared a lecture entitled "A Soviet View of American History." It proved a magnetic title. The student members of the Lecture Committee put posters up all over town and ran stories in the local newspapers. It was at the height of the Cold War. We expected a crowd for a big show on Monday evening, 29 October 1968.

On Sunday we had a major snowstorm, and Sunday evening about eight o'clock Jim Burns phoned me to say he had just received alarming news from Fursenko: He had said he was terribly sick and could not possibly give his speech; we must call the whole thing off. Fursenko was staying at the old Williams Inn, about four blocks from our house. Jim could not get into town, because Bee Hill Road, where he lived in an old farmhouse, was completely snowed in and he would not be plowed out until Monday. Would Anne and I go to the inn and find out what was the matter?

We put on our boots, and Anne, who was a registered nurse, took her kit with thermometer, stethoscope, and other useful articles. We found Fursenko in his underwear, lying prostrate on his bed in a small, overheated room with a pounding radiator. I introduced us and asked how he was feeling. "Feelink? I am dyink!" Anne asked if he had specific pain. "My legs ekk. My arms ekk. I am dyink." She took out a thermometer and asked him to open his mouth. He was suspicious, never having had his temperature taken that way. She explained what she was doing. She felt his pulse. She listened to his heart. She reported that everything was normal.

"What? I have no temperature? None at all? Well, let's go for a walk!" The dying man jumped up, put on his clothes and heavy boots. He was eager for a hike through the snow. It was a lovely, clear, starlit night, with the moon shining on snow-laden trees — several of them the white birches dear to all Russians. Anne turned to me and whispered, "You want my diagnosis? Here is one homesick, lonely, and scared Russian. Let's take him home with us."

Fursenko was glad to leave his lonely room. A Scotch, a good fire, and some light banter thawed him out considerably. It was clear that he was worried about the pending forum and all the publicity. He asked me how many people would be there and if I would please go over his speech. I did. It simply would not do. It was three times too long, and although there were some interesting points, too much of it was predictable, heavy Marxist historical analysis. I told him that in order to preserve its effectiveness, it should be drastically cut down and given sharper focus. I reminded him that he should leave time for questions and comments from our students. He was greatly relieved and asked if I would show him how to "fix it up." I reworked the text. About midnight, we went over it together and he went to bed happy.

On Monday evening the hall was packed; Fursenko's performance was impressive. He proved an intelligent and articulate advocate of his position and held his own in good-natured repartee. In the open discussion after the main presentation, a student asked him a loaded question, which he handled extremely well. Did he see any parallels, the student asked, between the U.S. invasion of Vietnam and the current Soviet invasion of Czechoslovakia? Fursenko said that in contrast to America, there is "no public outrage in the Soviet Union." Nevertheless, many Russians were bothered by it, especially writers and intellectuals. He concluded, "I hope we withdraw as soon as possible."

Fursenko stayed with us for two days. He was a delightful guest. He spoke warmly of his wife and helpmate, Natalia, and their children, two boys about the ages of our sons. We subsequently exchanged Christmas greetings and I tried, unsuccessfully, to telephone him when we visited Leningrad in 1974. In the intervening years, Fursenko became one of the most respected historians in the Soviet Union and a member of the prestigious Russian Academy of Science. Throughout the oppressive Stalin years he was able to keep alive the spirit of scholarly independence he had learned from his revered teacher, Boris Aleksandrovitch Romanov, who had encouraged students in Leningrad to follow historical evidence wherever it led.

When the secret Soviet archives were finally opened to scholars, Fursenko was able to use the material that enabled him, in 1997 with a colleague, to produce a truly important book: *"One Hell of a Gamble": Khrushchev, Castro and Kennedy and the Cuban Missile Crisis, 1958-1964*. The book has been well received. One reviewer wrote that it "has transformed our understanding of both sides in the Cold War. *One Hell of a Gamble* is one hell of a book."

"Dutchy" Wahl and His Wife's Pitcher

One of my favorite walks in Williamstown is the trail up Stone Hill, an old cart road that runs south of town and led, many years ago, to Pittsfield, Massachusetts.

This was also a favorite walk of a distinguished Williams professor of German, Georg Moritz Wahl. "Dutchy," as generations of his students called him with familiar affection, was born in pre-Imperial Germany and taught at Williams from 1892 until his retirement in 1917. He liked to sit on a crude bench at the top of Stone Hill and contemplate the lovely valley lying beneath him as he pondered the problems of his universe and mused over eternal verities, some of which he would expound in his volume *Maxims and Reflections on the Text of Life.*

The familiar old bench became known as Wahl's Stuhl. When it died of old age, shortly after its occupant's demise in 1924, students and townspeople took up a collection and, in 1926, erected a memorial stone bench with his name deeply inscribed. (A local citizen told me that he and others had contributed to apologize for the unjust way some townspeople had treated Dr. Wahl as a "German enemy" during the First World War.) I, along with hundreds of others, have blessed his memory as I rested on that solid expression of affection for an esteemed teacher.

One of Professor Wahl's few extravagances was to have kegs of dark German beer brewed for him in Troy, New York, and delivered to the dirt-floored cellar of his old frame house on Main Street. Every evening of his retirement years, he would take his wife's highly prized Meissen pitcher down the cellar stairs, draw a liter of beer and return slowly and precariously up the steep steps to sip his beer while pondering Ulrich von Hutten's use of the subjunctive mood in his third epistle to Desiderius Erasmus.

One evening, as the old gentleman started down the steps, he fell with a frightening crash. His wife hurried to the top of the stairs and cried into the darkness, "Georg! Georg! Is my pitcher broken?"

A long silence. Then another crash: "It iss *now,* by Gott!"

"Don't Send Me Your Walking Wounded" and a *Flight into Egypt*

After our boys graduated from Williamstown Elementary School, Anne served as school nurse for some twelve years. One year Peter returned from art school to spend his spring vacation at home. During that week, the art instructor of the kindergarten class became ill and Peter offered to fill in for a day or two. One of his charges scraped his knee during recess; his cries were loud, heartrending, and persistent. Peter calmed him down by saying that he was a brave little soldier and soldiers did not cry. Furthermore he would send him with a special, secret message to be delivered to the school nurse herself. The message read: "School Nurse, here is a casualty of the battlefield. Please repair and return. Art Instructor." Anne sent the soldier back to the instructor with a note: "Don't send me your walking wounded. Here are some extra Band-Aids. Anne Waite, R.N."

After retiring from her nursing duties, Anne became a docent at the Francine and Sterling Clark Art Institute in Williamstown. Under the knowledgeable and imaginative direction of Jock Brooks, associate director of the Clark and a specialist in impressionist art — which is one of the Clark's strong suits — the docents went through a rigorous training program. At weekly seminars each docent presented a paper on an artist and discussed with her colleagues how best to present his paintings to the children. I learned a great deal about art by serving as Anne's trial audience for her informal lectures.

On one occasion a Jewish mother complained to Anne that her son was being exposed to far too much Christian art. Anne said she would

79

show the mother a nice Jewish family. She took her and her son to see Peter Paul Rubens's *Flight into Egypt.*

As a docent's spouse, I joined in several of the "Artventures" Jock led to Europe. They included "The Art of Eastern Europe" (East Berlin, Dresden, Prague, Vienna, Budapest); "In the Steps of the Impressionists" (Paris, Giverny, Étretat, Honfleur); "The Art of Northern Europe" (St. Petersburg, Stockholm, Oslo, Copenhagen); "Art and Architecture of Southern France" (Arles, Carcassonne, Conques, Chartres).

SHOESHINE IN NEW ORLEANS

I was invited to give a paper on Hitler at the annual convention of the American Historical Association meeting in New Orleans in December 1972. Anne and I had never been there before and we decided to take a break from the Williamstown winter and stay on after the convention to enjoy the city and the climate.

To save money for other things, we moved out of the convention hotel and found comfortable lodgings in an old and attractive pension within long walking distance of the old city with its fine restaurants. My shoes had become a bit dirty and when a young street urchin said "Shine, sir?" I said sure and put my foot up on the rickety shinestand he had cobbled together from old pieces of two-by-fours. He was a bright-eyed black kid about nine years old; his kid brother, about six, stood at one side, watching. "Oh, those are mighty fine shoes you got there, sir," he said, "Just feel that leather! Mighty fine leather in them shoes! Yes, sir . . . You know, sir, just from feeling that leather, I can tell you 'xactly where you got them shoes. Yes, sir, I can tell you the city, the street, and the store where you got them shoes!"

Since I had got them some years before in Boston, I thought that was highly unlikely, so I said, "No, son, I don't believe that you can!" He replied, "Oh, yes, sir, I can! And I'll bet you a one-dollar bill that I can!" I thought for a minute, and since I am a person who believes in miracles — I'm a sucker for amazing gadgets and gizmos advertised in the back of magazines — I asked him to repeat his bet. He said, "I'm bettin' I can tell you the city, street, and store where you got them shoes." I said I'd take the bet and held out a dollar bill. He said, "Jimmie, show the gent'man the color of our money." Jimmie rattled a few coins around in his cupped hands. And I said, "Now tell me about my shoes." He said: "You got them shoes in New Orleans, Louisiana, and you got 'em on Baker Street and in front of Louis XIV Antique Store. That's where you got them shoes — I didn't say where you purchased them, that's where you *got* 'em!" Little Jimmie looked at me apprehensively; I laughed and said, "Well, I guess you *got* me!" and handed him his dollar plus a twenty-five-cent tip.

It may not have been the best shoeshine I ever received, but it was certainly the most enjoyable.

WILLIAMS IN CHINA
WITH FIRST-CLASS TWIDDLERS

In January 1980, not long after the end of the Cultural Revolution, Anne and I accompanied a group of Williams students on a month's trip to the People's Republic of China.

At an organizational meeting prior to the trip, we discussed what we might take along as a goodwill gesture to Chinese children — some small souvenir from America. It had to be something that had no political significance, that we could carry in great quantity, and that would be inexpensive. One student had the happy idea that we should take "smiley buttons" — those cheerful, bright-eyed little yellow faces on metal buttons to be pinned on clothing.

A good idea, but where to find them in abundance? No merchant in Williamstown or the neighboring towns could supply them. John Hyde, another faculty member who was going with us and who had recently served as dean of the college, was planning to take the bus to New York and said he was sure he could find some smiley buttons in one of the many novelty shops near the Port Authority bus terminal. He found himself on Forty-Second Street gazing intently into novelty shop windows that were displaying all manner of raunchy sexual devices. Suddenly a Williams undergraduate hailed him cheerily: "Hi, Dean Hyde, what are you doing here?" Hyde knew that he couldn't possibly say "I'm just looking for smiley buttons" — he could hear their response: "Yeah, sure, sir."

There was no satisfactory way out; so he just turned and walked away.

We did manage to assemble a large supply of the buttons, and they were a huge success.

One of our first stops was at the University of Zhongxian, where I talked with the chairman of the history department. He had received his Ph.D. from the University of Washington and, prior to the Cultural Revolution, had taught European history. During that horrendous period, the Red Guards had destroyed all his books, forced him out of his position, and required him to undergo a program of humiliation and torture they called "reeducation." For three years he hoed potatoes on a farm. He had been reinstated in his position but had trouble teaching European history with only a few old textbooks. When I returned to Williamstown, I sent him several cartons of books collected from my colleagues. I do not know whether they ever reached him.

We visited many kindergartens and found the children beguiling. In every school they played the same game — tug-of-war. We got the point almost at once: Young Communists all pull together. At one school an earnest little boy who couldn't have been more than five played a very creditable violin solo and three young girls danced a delightful ballet to welcome us. At another school the children sang, in our honor, a song they had learned in English. We were enchanted:

Low, low, low your boat
gently down the stleam,
mellily, mellily, mellily, mellily
life is but a dleam.

John Hyde, who plays by ear, saw an accordion and suggested that it was our turn to entertain them. Our group of students and faculty joined in a robust version of "Old MacDonald Had a Farm," with enthusiastic "oink-oink heres" and "quack-quack theres" and "moo-moo here, moo-moo, theres." The kids were delighted with our performance. One little girl asked, "How could one falmer have a whole falm all to himself?" A bright-eyed boy replied positively, "He was big capitalist. Name of MacDonald Hambulgel."

At a hospital in Changsha we were asked if we would like to see an operation conducted under acupuncture. We would. As in every institution we visited, whether kindergarten, factory, collective farm, or hospital, we first were invited to meet with the person in authority (school principal, farm director, factory supervisor, senior doctor). Over many mugs of China tea the person in charge explained the procedures, problems, and accomplishments of his institution. In the hospital, the person making the presentation was an elderly physician who spoke very good English, having received his training during the 1930s at Cornell University Medical School. He explained, as much as it is possible, the mysteries of acupuncture. Several needles would be used, depending on the medical problem, and to the needles there was attached a copper wire that was given a mild charge of electricity to agitate the needles and thus stimulate them into doing whatever it is they do.

This morning, he said, we had a choice of watching either open heart surgery or a hysterectomy. No patient is obliged to undergo acupuncture. The two female patients, both peasant women, had chosen it because it was the traditional practice in their villages. They knew that they would be given no anesthesia, only a mild relaxant.

Anne, who had experience as an operating-room nurse, and I joined the group who were to watch the heart surgery. We were ushered up to a small spectators' gallery over the operation theater; the Chinese doctor sat at my side. I think of this experience whenever someone says, "That was unbelievably pretty" or something was "unbelievably funny." What I was about to see was, in the most literal sense, unbelievable. My mind simply could not accept what my eyes saw.

The patient's chest cavity had already been opened. We could see her beating heart. The patient was conscious. She looked up at the circle of observers above her and gently waved her fingers in greeting. Several students took pictures of the scene.

At that moment the lights in the operating theater blew a fuse. The physician at my side said, "Not to worry, it often happens." Three nurses shone flashlights onto the field of operation. I whispered to the physician, "But what about the charge of electricity that was agitating the

"Not to worry! Anesthetists are first-class twiddlers."

needles?" Again the confidant answer, "Not to worry! Anesthetists are first-class twiddlers."

I made Anne promise that if I ever needed open-heart surgery in China, she would make darn sure I had first-class twiddlers.

In a government Medical Supply Center, Anne purchased an acupuncture kit of the kind sent out by the thousands to remote Chinese villages. I still have it. The kit contains one ten-inch rubberized mannequin whose body is marked with dozens of red pinpoints, each with its own tiny Chinese character, presumably showing the places to insert the very thin needles also included in the kit. The human ear must be especially sensitive, for included in the kit is a separate pink, rubberized, rather more than life-size plastic ear. As I examine it now, I can count more than sixty places where needles may be inserted. Two pages of instructions are given in Chinese. They are apparently sufficient to perform acupuncture. I have not been tempted to try.

One clear and cold Saturday morning, I was walking down a broad boulevard in Guilin when I noticed two Red Army soldiers approaching. The officer — the man with a ballpoint pen in his chest pocket — smiled and nodded a greeting. After they had passed me, they came back, overtook me, and the officer asked amiably, "Excuse me, sir, would you please speak English with me?" I said I would be delighted to. Thus began my experience of the way totalitarian government crushes personal relations.

He asked me how I was enjoying China and if there were anything he could do to make my stay more pleasant. Anything at all. Well, I said, as a matter of fact, there was something that would be very helpful. I had lost the little screw that held the arm of my glasses on its hinge — I was temporarily using a paper clip — and wondered if I could find a proper screw at an oculist's shop. He said he was native to Guilin, he was home on leave and had the morning free, and if I were free for the morning, he would enjoy showing me something of the city while look-ing with me for an oculist. We visited several shops before finding one that could repair my glasses. His military friend, who spoke no English, left us. We both enjoyed a simple but excellent lunch. He told me about his family and talked guardedly about his hopes of finding more freedom after his stint in the army. He wanted to be a teacher. Perhaps, he laughed, he might even become a teacher of English. I encouraged him and told him his English was very good indeed. He was trying to learn the language by listening to the Voice of America, which his government was then encouraging, and reading American cowboy stories. He was a particular fan of Zane Grey. He finally worked up the courage to ask me if I could possibly send him some Zane Grey novels. I said I would be glad to. He wrote his mailing address in my little pocket diary and I gave him my address. He said he looked forward so much to communicating with me. We continued our pleasant conversation while walking back to the vicinity of my hotel. Both of us expressed our pleasure at having met and our hope of continuing our new-found friendship. We bid each other a warm goodbye. I liked him immensely.

That evening I suddenly felt quite ill, feverish and vomiting. I went directly to bed, telling the students in the adjacent room that I did not want to be disturbed.

About nine o'clock a student opened my door a crack, said he was terribly sorry to disturb me, but this was an emergency. A soldier had come up the service stairs and said that he simply must see me. It was my officer friend. He looked frightened and deeply embarrassed. He could hardly look at me; he kept shaking his head and taking very deep breaths. I invited him to sit down. He said he couldn't. He paced back and forth and finally said that he was so sorry, so very sorry, but he must ask me not to send him those books from America. He really should not receive them. I said I understood — though I was not sure that I did. Then he said he must make another request that made him very sad, very sad. He said, "It's your little book!"

It finally dawned on me what was so heavily on his mind. I went to the closet, found my pocket diary, tore out the page on which he had written his address and handed it to him. He thanked me and started to weep. Again he said he was sorry, thanked me again and again, said he must leave at once, shook my hand and went down the back stairs. I never heard from him again.

He had taken a great personal risk by going at night to an American's hotel. He was compelled to do so because if the "authorities" had found his name and address in his own handwriting in an American's private diary, his whole career might have been put in jeopardy. Such was life in the People's Republic of China.

I had expressed a desire to attend church service Sunday morning and asked if there was a Protestant church in Shanghai. Our Communist tour director said she thought there was but she discouraged me from going, saying it would not be worth the effort, that only a few old women would be there. I said it was important to me, that I wanted to go, and that three or four others would join me. Could she please order a cab? She called her supervisor. In about ten minutes an unsmiling man arrived. He would go with us as a guide — less to help us, I suspected, than to report on what took place during a Christian service.

We arrived at an enormous brick church, built, we later discovered, by the Methodists in the 1930s. We were in for a surprise. There must have been well over 1,000 worshipers who filled the huge sanctuary and the extensive gallery that encircled it. As we started up the stairs to the gallery, a friendly Chinese woman in her late seventies came down the stairs to welcome us in English, saying she could find us individual seats. We separated. She ushered me to a seat and told me that the pastor had chosen his text from Paul's letters to the churches in Rome and in Corinth — showing me the texts in her Chinese Bible (Cor. I:1, 2 3 and Rom. 1:16).

From my seat overlooking the congregation I could see that the church was packed with people of all ages, including many young parents with their children. For three quarters of an hour the young preacher held his congregation riveted. He held them not only because of his fervor, but by his daring. I understood only one word in the sermon, but it was crucial. It came from Paul's letter to the church in Corinth: "I preach Christ crucified. Others preach different doctrine . . . but I preach Christ crucified." He repeated that phrase. He then quoted Paul's letter to the Romans: "For I am not ashamed of the Gospel: it is the power of God for salvation to everyone who has faith." (Romans 1:16)

He then announced the final hymn. The organ and its pipes, along with stained-glass windows, had been smashed by the Red Guards, but a piano played the music of the magnificent old Protestant hymn, "Beneath the Cross of Jesus." The congregation, of course, sang in Chinese; I knew the first verse and sang in English. As I sang I could hear it being sung in languages I understood. Behind me on my right was a tall, handsome black singing in French; behind me on my left was a young mother with her towheaded son singing in German. To hear the same hymn being sung in different tongues in such a setting was for me inspiring:

Beneath the cross of Jesus, I fain would take my stand,
The shadow of a mighty rock within a weary land;
A home within the wilderness, a rest beyond the way,
From the burning of the noontime heat, and the burden of the day.

I introduced myself to the two nearby singers. The man was from Guinea and was studying medicine at the university. The woman was from East Berlin and her husband was teaching physics at the university. She said she and her son came every Sunday, and every Sunday both services (at 8:30 and at 10:00) were filled.

As the crowd moved toward the door, I noticed a huge copper cauldron being filled with contributions. The elderly lady met me again and asked if I would like to talk to the pastor, who was her son. I said I would. Three of us from the Williams group were joined by the stony-faced "guide" who had been assigned to us. We met in what had previously been a Sunday school room, now commandeered for secular elementary school rooms. Pictures of Jesus had been replaced with those of Mao Zedong and Deng Xiaoping. The elderly woman introduced me to her husband, now the retired pastor of the church, and to their son, the present pastor, and his wife. Both of the older people had studied at a Methodist seminary in upstate New York in the 1930s and remarked that this was the first time they had spoken English in over forty years. I congratulated their son on his inspiring sermon and — feeling like a first-century Christian coming from Ephesus to Corinth — I said that as a deacon of the church, I brought them greetings from First Congregational Church in Williamstown. Toward the close of a rewarding conversation, I asked if there were any way our church could be helpful to them. The pastor looked at our "guide" and cut me off rather abruptly. "No, thank you, nothing at all. Please send us nothing but your love." As usual, it took me a little time to figure out the reasons for his answer: Their church was already strong and growing; they did not want the Communist authorities to accuse them of receiving money from a capitalist country.

On the cab ride back to the hotel, we experienced something amazing. The intense Communist "guide" gave us, in broken but enthusiastic English, a complete résumé of the sermon we had heard in Chinese.

At our farewell dinner in Beijing, I received an ornate certificate whose wording I view with ambivalence. Among other things, it was occasioned, perhaps, by watching me do needlepoint. (I'll talk about my hobby later.)

This award acknowledges the contributions of

R. G. L. Waite

To the growing relationship between
The United States of America and the People's Republic of China
By rivalling the Great Wall as an object of Chinese curiosity.

January 1980

Deacon of the Church
"I'll Be Seeing You"

I am an ordained deacon of the First Congregational Church of Williamstown. This position has bestowed upon me some benefits that are certainly not described in our church documents of 1765.

I recall one Sunday morning going early to put the numbers on the hymn board, when I saw Daniel O'Connor, chairman of the Williams philosophy department, coming down from our church choir loft. I found that surprising, because I knew that though Dan has a fine voice, he is also a devout Catholic and I assumed any singing in a choir that he did was in St. Patrick's Church. I met him at the door and asked if he were backsliding or forward-jumping. He smiled and wished me good morning.

During the next week we celebrated the memorial service of Carl Pepper, a great guy with a fine sense of fun who had sung in our choir. During his professional career he had been a lead singer in a nightclub. At the service I noted that Daniel O'Connor was to sing a solo that was not often heard at funerals, "I'll Be Seeing You."

I had not known that that particular song had been Carl's favorite; indeed, his signature song, the last one he sang at the close of his nightclub program. You remember the words:

I'll be seeing you in all the old familiar places,
Everything my heart embraces all day through. . .

In every lovely summer's day,

In everything that's bright and gay,
I'll always think of you that way.

I'll see you in the morning sun
And when the day is through,
I'll be looking at the moon,
But I'll be seeing you.

I also had not known that it was totally appropriate for Carl's memorial service when sung a cappella in his good friend Dan's rich baritone.

As a deacon, I was especially rewarded by a sermon preached by John C. Bennett, Willliams '24, who had sometimes attended our church as an undergraduate. Dr. Bennett had become a distinguished theologian who would serve as president of the Union Theological Seminary. He was a fine preacher who had, unfortunately, a pronounced facial tic. When he came to an important part of his discourse, he would throw back his head and forcibly close his left eye in what was, in fact, an obvious wink.

It was Communion Sunday in April 1956 when Bennett preached at our church. As a deacon who would serve the elements, I was sitting with my colleagues — all males in those days — in the front row of the sanctuary. Bennett was preaching from the Gospel according to St. John about the woman who had been taken in adultery. He asked the congregation the following rhetorical question, "And what did Jesus actually *say* to that fallen woman?" At that point, the preacher was seized by his tic. And at that juncture, I'm sorry to say, Deacon Waite did the unforgivable. He burst out laughing. His colleagues joined him and we then were unable to stop. It was awful.

Paul Tillich, the eminent religious thinker, also came to Williamstown in 1956 when he preached in the college chapel on his current interest, St. Paul's Letter to the Romans. After the sermon, he accepted our invitation to eat with us in the church's Fellowship Hall and to participate in a discussion of his sermon. During the discussion period, a woman who shall remain nameless — because I really have forgotten her name — and who had been reading a famous best-seller, asked Dr. Tillich if he didn't think that Norman Vincent Peale was "the greatest theologian in the world."

Paul Tillich was a fine and gentle man who did not want to hurt the woman's feelings. He was rendered absolutely speechless by her question and simply did not know how to respond to her. After a long pause, someone in the audience — oh, how I wish it had been I — said, "I think Dr. Tillich finds Paul a-Pealing, and Peale a-Pauling."

My father would have loved it.

Interview with
the Governor General of Canada

One morning at Williams in 1952, I received a letter with the happy news that Harvard University Press planned to publish my doctoral thesis on the German Free Corps Movement — more about that in a minute. Professor Richard A. Newhall, the senior Europeanist at Williams who had read the thesis, noticed that it involved a certain British Colonel Alexander, who, Newhall suspected, was the present Governor General of Canada. Perhaps I should drive up to Government House, Ottawa, to visit His Excellency. This conversation inspired my first research trip for my first book.

Harold Rupert Leofric George Alexander, First Earl of Tunis, was, by far, the most distinguished soldier I had ever met. Born in County Tyrone, Ireland, and educated at Sandhurst, he commanded a battalion of Irish Guards on the western front during the First World War. In the Second World War he commanded a corps in rear-guard action during the Dunkirk evacuation of 1940. He was the last British soldier to leave France. After serving in Burma, he was made Commander-in-Chief of Allied Forces in the Middle East. He personally commanded troops in North Africa, winning at Tunis what has been called "one of the most complete victories in military history" — hence his title — and the appointment as Supreme Allied Commander of the Mediterranean Theater. From 1952 to 1954 he served as Governor General of Canada.

My professional interest in Lord Alexander stemmed from his experience of the years 1919–1920, when he became directly involved in the Baltic area with volunteer German troops called the *Freikorps* or Free

Corps. For reasons I'll explain later, I had entitled my dissertation about these troops "Vanguard of Nazism." I knew from their privately published memoirs that they had direct dealings with Lord Alexander and I wanted to talk with him about it before my manuscript was published.

First, let me say briefly how Alexander got involved with the *Freikorps*. These battle-tough German veterans of the Great War had been sent to the Baltic to fight the advancing Red Army, which was bent on following Lenin's orders to advance revolution in Europe "on the points of the Red Army's bayonets." That threat alarmed the Allies, but after the sacrifices of the Great War, they had no stomach for sending their own troops to stop the Red advance. Someone had the bright idea of sending the German volunteers to do Allied work for them. After the Germans stopped the Red advance, the Allies thanked them kindly and told them to disband and go home. But the *Freikorps* had other ideas. They wanted to use the Baltic as a staging area for overthrowing the despised Weimar Republic — those "Weimar Traitors" who, they believed, had "stabbed the German Army in the back" and betrayed the Fatherland by signing the Armistice and the hated "Versailles-Diktat." They refused to disband and kept making excuses for keeping their corps together so they could march on Berlin and establish a military dictatorship.

This is where Alexander came in. Fed up with Free Corps stalling and alarmed by their political ambitions, the Allies sent then Colonel Alexander as head of a military mission to make sure these German formations were disbanded. That is why I wanted to talk to Lord Alexander about his personal experience with the *Freikorps*.

I wrote to the Governor General, explaining my book project, noting his important part in it and asking if I might have an interview. I received a letter in reply written by his aide-de-camp, a certain Major General Letson, as I recall, saying that His Excellency was at the moment in London, attending His Majesty, and would not be returning to Government House until the first week of September. The letter concluded with a memorable example of British understatement. Letson, who had been Alexander's aide for at least a decade, wrote: "Meanwhile,

96

I venture to say that I am reasonably sure that the former Colonel Alexander mentioned in your correspondence is, indeed, His Excellency."

I wrote to General Letson, thanking him for his prompt and courteous reply and saying that it just so happened that my wife and I were motoring to Ottawa during the second week in September, and wondering if His Excellency might be able to see me. Within a fortnight I received an official British Government telegram saying that His Excellency the Governor General of Canada would be pleased to receive Professor Robert G. L. Waite at Government House, 11 o'clock on 16 September 1952.

We packed camping equipment in our old Chevrolet and with our two boys, at that time aged four and one, started north for Ottawa by way of Vermont. We crossed the border into Canada at an infrequently used station. The kindly Scots official asked me, "And what is the nature of your mission in Ottawa?" I said that I was going to talk with His Excellency the Governor General. He looked at my two-day growth of beard, old flannel shirt, and the generalized chaos in the back seat and said slyly, "Oh, aye. I tell you, lad, we ha' His Majesty King George VI in the back room playing poker with the lads, would ya care for a hand?" I took the official British Government telegram from my pocket and showed it to him. He said reverently, "Well, I will indeed be damned."

In Ottawa the government had made reservations for the Governor General's guests in the Lord Elgin Hotel. Our suite of rooms was immediately over the suite recently occupied by the late premier, William Lyon Mackenzie King.

At the appointed hour, I was driving slowly up the manicured driveway to Government House when the tailpipe and muffler fell halfway off the car and banged along the crushed stone to announce our arrival. I asked Anne to sneak it out of there and have it fixed while I was talking with the Governor General. Good sport as always, she drove it to a garage and, while the car was being repaired, took the kids to watch the logjams in the Ottawa River. Meanwhile, at the entrance of Government House I was met by General Letson in full uniform, complete with medal-bedecked chest, swagger stick, and walrus mustache, but friendly withal. He accompanied me to the Governor General's office and introduced us. It was an impressive office. Rubbed cypress-paneled walls held large, signed portraits of the royal family and pictures of Alexander with Eisenhower, Montgomery, and other World War II commanders. I was struck with the irony: Here I was, a former subcorporal, meeting with the commanding general of all Allied troops in the Mediterranean theater.

Lord Alexander was a relatively short, trimly built soldier who was greatly admired by both the Allied troops he had commanded and by the Germans he disbanded. Their privately printed memoirs — copies of which Alexander lent me ("Not much good, written in German you know") — expressed their admiration and respect for him as a *Frontsoldat*, which from them was high praise indeed. He was friendly and gracious to me. He asked me to sit down and offered me a cigarette — imprinted with his family coat of arms. He asked me about my war experience, saying that he understood I was "a soldier too." It did not take long to tell him. He was trying to put me at ease. In that, he utterly failed.

His response to my first question was so completely incongruous with the formality of the impressive setting and the stature of the man standing before me that he left me flabbergasted. Our conversation went something like this:

> *He:* Yes, Professor Waite, let me see, the *Freikorps*. Yes, the *Freikorps*. Haven't thought of them in years. How can I be helpful? What would you like to know?
>
> *I:* Well, sir, I should like to know your reaction to some of the leading figures you dealt with personally. What, for example, did you think of Karlis Ulmanis, president of Latvia?
>
> *He:* Ulmanis, ah, yes, Ulmanis. I found him a bit of a shit. You know?

I knew, all right; I just didn't know what to say. I suppose if I had been a Brit I might have responded nonchalantly, "Quite!"

GERMANY AND MY OLD UNCLE HARRY

There was great excitement in the Waite household when we learned that we would soon be spending our first year abroad doing research on Adolf Hitler in Germany. Our final destination would be Munich, but since I needed to work in the British Library (then still the British Museum Library) and in the Wiener Library in London, a private library with valuable holdings on the Hitler period, we would go early and spend a week or two in England. I would be able to meet the wonderful relatives who had sent their impoverished Canadian relatives the magical "English Box" all those Christmases ago.

I also learned that Bob Branson was on the Associated Press desk in London. I would certainly look him up. Branson was a Williams graduate who had served as war correspondent in the Pacific during the Second World War. He had been badly shaken up and, to get him back on his feet, the college hired him to work in the publicity office. He, too, had some English relatives, and we enjoyed telling ribald stories in a broad "English" accent, a phony concoction of North Country, Midlands, and Cockney.

When we arrived in London, we took a room on the third floor of a small hotel on Gower Street, within walking distance of the British Museum. Anne and the boys took off to stay with Auntie Dot in Bournemouth, leaving me to my research. After a few days alone, I thought it would be fun to have dinner with Branson; I rang him at the AP desk. He worked odd hours, so I left a message for him to ring me back. A half hour later the phone rang in the hall of my hotel, a heavily accented voice asked, "Eh, is this Bub? This is your old Uncle 'arry."

Knowing full well that it was Branson, and probably after a drink, I answered with jocular enthusiasm: "Not me old Uncle 'arry! Well, 'ow the 'ell are you, 'arry? Eh? 'ow *are* you? . . . 'ow are they 'angin', 'arry?"

The phone was silent for at least sixty ghastly seconds. Then a gentle and confused voice said, "Bob, this is your old Uncle 'arry, your mother's older brother, you know. They tell me you 'ave a car. I wonder if you'd like to drive up to Bedford Sunday next and 'ave a cup of tea with us — we're 'aving a bit of a family reunion."

It was, indeed, my old Uncle Harry. Never in my life have I more deeply regretted something I have said. I had looked forward eagerly to meeting my mother's family, for I wanted to express my gratitude for the consistent kindness and generosity the Carter family had shown us and how much it meant to us all. I also wanted to let them know how grateful Mother had been for their supportive letters during some pretty rough sledding. Instead, in my first verbal contact, I had come across as a brash young smart aleck who made vulgar remarks and ridiculed their language. And my Uncle Harry, of all people!

Harry Carter was the senior and most respected member of the family. A self-made man who had earned his way to the board of directors of a Bedford bank, he was also a board member of several charities and an elder in the Methodist Church. He looked the part in his carefully brushed dark suit, starched white shirt, conservative tie with his grandfather's stickpin, his invariably shined black shoes, derby hat, meticulously furled umbrella, and Methodist prayer book. One did not ask Harry Carter how they were 'angin'.

Thanks to Anne and our two boys, I survived an awkward Sunday afternoon and we started to plan for the year ahead in Munich.

THE HIGH COMMISSIONER OF GERMANY:
"I'd Rather Not Talk About It."

Soon after our arrival in Munich, we, along with the other Senior Fulbright Research Scholars and their spouses, received an invitation to meet with Dr. James B. Conant, the High Commissioner of Germany, in Bonn.

We were delighted to get the invitations because Anne and I knew the Conants quite well. While he was president of Harvard University, Mr. Conant, a former professor of chemistry, had designed a course in the history of science for nonscientists as part of his general-education program. He had assigned essays in the course and wanted to have them read by a historian who was a nonscientist to help him evaluate the papers. The chairman of the history department recommended me because, I assumed, of my ignorance of things scientific.

I read the essays and Mr. Conant invited me to the President's House to discuss them over tea. Since there were a great many papers, we met on Thursdays for a couple of weeks. During the 1920s Conant had studied chemistry in Germany and was interested in my research on the *Freikorps.*

Anne had known Mrs. Conant because of their mutual involvement in the Harvard Dames, a tony name for an informal group of women whose husbands were graduate students.

In Bonn that afternoon a long line of distinguished people waited to be received by the High Commissioner and his wife. When our turn came, the Conants engaged us in a lively conversation that annoyed the German aide who was trying to keep the line moving.

At this point I must interrupt the story to introduce my good friend from Williams, the late Harlan — "Harpo" to everyone — Hanson, professor of Germanic studies. I can't think of Harpo without smiling. A *bon vivant* of Falstaffian girth and temperament, a man of erudition and a delightful companion with a bubbling sense of devilment, he was born and raised in Wisconsin and became a lifelong rooter for the Green Bay Packers. At the close of his memorial service at Williams, the gothic chapel resounded with his triumphant recessional: "On, Wisconsin. On, Wisconsin. . ." Harpo would have loved it.

We had worked closely together on a translation for the Harvard Press of Erich Eyck's two-volume *Geschichte der Weimarer Republik* — he doing most of the work. We had also laughed together about our similar military careers during World War II. The only military citation either of us was entitled to wear was the Good Conduct Medal — commonly called the "Ruptured Duck" for its awkwardly rendered brass eagle design, and handed out by the thousands to all soldiers who had stayed out of trouble for a year.

The award was not much, but Harpo made the most of it. He had a metalsmith make us lapel medals that resembled an award of genuine distinction such as the Croix de Guerre. Whenever anyone saw our lapel bars, and remarked that he had never seen the Good Conduct Medal appear in such a distinguished form, Harpo's reply was typical: "Precisely."

At the High Commissioner's reception in Germany, where I was wearing my award, an impressive-appearing German with some sort of ribbon across his chest asked me about my "order." I thought of Harpo and replied with absolute truth, "It's nothing . . . I'd rather not talk about it." As I walked slowly away, affecting a slight limp, I heard him remark to a colleague, *"Welche Bescheidenheit!"* (What modesty!)

When I told the story to Harpo, he insisted on buying me a drink.

OTTOBRUNN BEI MÜNCHEN:
Hans and Käthe Thomamüller and Four Kinds of Kraut

Back to Munich. Since my interest was in the Nazi period, the place to start was in the *Institut für Zeitgeschichte* (Institute for Contemporary History). This research center, library, and archive had originally been called Institute for Research into the Causes of National Socialism and had been established shortly after the war with financial support from both the Bavarian and the Federal Governments with the laudable purpose of trying to understand causes of National Socialism in an effort to assure that such a catastrophe would never be repeated.

I soon discovered that there was absolutely no hope of finding a furnished flat for an American couple with two children in still badly bombed and shelled metropolitan Munich. The best we could do was a *Häuschen* in the little village of Ottobrunn, about seven miles southeast of Munich on the Rosenheimerlandstrasse.

The little cottage had electricity, a kitchen with cold running water, living room with space heater, an unheated bedroom, and a cellar with the washing facilities in the form of a huge copper kettle over a tiny wood stove. We hired Frau Rest, an indefatigable *Putzfrau* who cleaned the house, did the laundry, scrubbed the steps, and, at the end of a long day, insisted on scything the grass "to get the kinks out of my back."

The best thing about the cottage was our wonderful neighbors, Käthe and Hans Thomamüller. As a teenager Hans had been a volunteer in the Great War and recalled having met Field Marshal Paul von Hindenburg. The great man had given him a cigar. During the revolutionary upheaval in Munich in 1918–1919, Hans first joined the

Communist Red Guards and then the Von Epp *Freikorps*, which subsequently joined one of Hitler's Storm Troops. Since I had written on this period in German history, I profited greatly from the many talks we had together. During World War II, Hans had served in the *Wehrmacht* and lost both of his hands in trying to rescue a comrade from a high-tension wire. His kind and gentle disposition and beguiling humor were belied by a terrifying appearance. He wore a hook on one arm, his dark beard invariably showed dried blood from Käthe's ineffective efforts to shave him with a straightedge, his eyes were bloodshot from too much beer. Altogether, he looked like a sinister Captain Hook. Yet our son Peter, then three years old, saw through outward appearances and took to him at once. Peter spent happy hours playing in the Thomamüllers' cozy kitchen. Especially he looked forward to four o'clock in the afternoon, when their clock cuckooed four times, for that was when Hans would sing his little ditty:

Peter, es ist noch vier,
Wo ist mein Bier?

Peter would go down the steep steps to the mysterious cellar and bring up the first of several bottles of dark Bavarian beer delivered weekly by donkey cart from the Ottobrunn brewery, "established in the year 927."

The Thomamüllers had no television or radio. But Peter loved to draw at their kitchen table, and Hans would suggest subjects. While he drew, Käthe would tell him simple children's stories in German, and in one way and another Peter learned to converse with them. Käthe's father had been huntmaster for the Wittelsbachs, the royal house of Bavaria, and their wide-eaved, colorfully stenciled house was festooned with horns from dozens of deer, chamois, and mountain goats. They also kept Spitzberger dogs and fed them candy. After the dogs got fat and died, a taxidermist cousin converted them into scatter rugs, which Peter carefully jumped over. One summer evening after I had spanked Peter for being disobedient, he opened the casement window of his downstairs bedroom, dressed himself for the first time, lowered himself to the

Peter, es ist noch vier,
Wo ist mein Bier?

ground, and, grasping his security blanket, ran across the yard to the Thomamüllers. He told them, "It's safer in your house."

Käthe became Anne's close friend. She took Anne on her daily shopping trips to the many little shops in the village and introduced her to the proprietors. This produced something of an embarrassment, because Käthe insisted on using Anne's full title: "Frau Professor Doktor Waite"; this meant that every day thereafter each proprietor, calling off the full ticket, insisted that she come to the front of the line — blue jeans or no — since she outranked every other *Hausfrau* in Ottobrunn.

One other American couple lived in the village, a U.S. Army sergeant and his wife. Sergeant David Hammond commuted to McGraw Kaserne, a huge Air Corps base nearby. Claire Hammond offered to buy us supplies from the PX, but we were determined to live on the German economy. We permitted one exception. On a warm summer day, Sergeant Hammond offered to take our sons to the PX to treat them to an American ice-cream cone. Both boys were dressed in complete Bavarian *Trachten: Lederhosen* with *Hosenträgern,* knee socks, and *Halbschuhe.* Peter, who was very blond, was often photographed in Munich as a "real German," since most native kids were wearing American blue jeans.

When Sergeant Hammond drove up to the barracks gate, the soldier on guard said, "You know damn well, Hammond, you can't bring those Kraut kids in here." Three-year-old Peter said, *"Was soll Kraut heissen?"* (What is Kraut supposed to mean?) Geoffrey, with the superior knowledge of a seven-year-old replied, *"Weiss-du dass nicht? Es gibt drei Sorten: Weiss, Rot, und Sauer.* (Don't you know? There are three kinds: white, red, and sour). The guard said, "See? What did I tell you? Get those Kraut kids out of here!" Sergeant Hammond turned to Geoff: "For heaven's sake, Geoff, tell him who you are!" He did and they got their cones.

There were two automobiles in Ottobrunn: the dentist's prewar diesel Mercedes and my new Ford Consul, which took me every day to the *Institut für Zeitgeschichte* or to the University in Munich. In our village there lived a very attractive young widow whose husband had been killed fighting the Russians. (It seemed to me that the war casualties had all taken place on the Eastern Front.) Frau Witwe Kronsdorf had obtained some sort of job in the city and needed a ride. I offered to take her, since public transportation was still uncertain in 1953. There was a great deal of reconstruction in the city, with many detours and one-way streets, and I got lost. I turned to my passenger and thought I had said, "I'm sorry, Mrs. Kronsdorf, but I have got us lost." She smiled seductively and said, *"Leider, mein Herr, dass haben Sie noch nicht getan."* (Unfortunately, sir, you have not done that yet!)

I thought it an inappropriate response and began to reconsider what I had said. About midnight I figured out that I had used the wrong verb. *Sich verfahren* means to lose one's way; *verführen* means to seduce. In saying *"Es tut mir Leid, Frauwidwe, aber Ich habe Sie verführt,"* I had actually said, "I'm sorry that I have seduced you." I told Anne about my mistake and her surprising response. The next day she made arrangements for the young widow to find alternative transportation.

Two special events marked our last week in Ottobrunn. Anne and I held our first and our last *Bierabend.* Since so many people in the village had been kind to us, we invited a rather large group in for a social evening. The impulse was good, but I had failed to appreciate the important role status and marital rank played in social relations in a rural German village. Wives took the titles and shared the social distinctions enjoyed by their husbands. Thus, "Frau Veterinarian Doctor Schmidt" outranked "Frau Blacksmith Mittlersheim," and "Frau Streetcar Conductor Meyerhof" outranked "Frau Streetcar Motorman Weiskopf." Many of the wives we invited to our party had not met each other socially, were uncertain about how to address each other or where to sit — not wishing to commit the faux pas of sitting in a preferred place, such as the chair next to the hostess or in the middle of the sofa. Consequently, the party was going nowhere very slowly. Anne, realizing she had to get things rolling, thought she could comment safely on the miserable weather by saying in her careful German that the air was misty this evening, so she said very slowly and distinctly, *"Guten Abend, meine Damen und Herren. Die Luft Heute Abend ist voll von Mist, nicht wahr?"*

The difficulty was that the word "mist" means something quite different in German. She had actually said that the air was filled with barnyard manure. That posed problems for our guests. Because Anne held the highest status among all the wives at the party, they felt obliged to accept the pronouncement she had made. Their job was to figure out why this condition existed. Käthe solved the problem by asserting, "Yes, indeed! The Frau Professor Doktor is, of course, quite correct. I myself saw with my own eyes the shepherd passing by our street this afternoon."

Just before we were to leave Ottobrunn, the Thomamüllers invited us to a farewell dinner. Käthe had really gone flat out preparing a "real Bavarian meal." First we had clear chicken soup surrounding an enormous potato dumpling, then cucumber salad, then trout; that was followed by Wienerschnitzel with potato salad and rolls, then venison with gravy and bread dumpling, and finally fruit and cake for dessert. The proportions were immense and Käthe kept urging us to eat more. All was washed down with water glasses of *Kalte Ente* — chilled white wine laced with brandy. We were all stuffed well beyond our gills. Then Hans got up and made a gracious and generous speech that ended with an alarming proposition.

He spoke of how our two nations had suffered in warring against each other and how good it was to live in peace with each other; he also said how much he and his wife had enjoyed our children and how much Anne's friendship meant to Käthe. Then he filled two liter steins with dark beer. One of those steins, he said, had belonged to his grandfather and he wanted me to keep it. Then he asked me to stand and, with tears in his eyes, said that "despite the great social difference between us," he proposed that we go on a *du* relationship; that is, that we use informal "you" and our first names in talking with each other. The ceremony required that we link arms and chugalug the entire liter of beer. Given the condition of my stomach, that was something I was physically unable to do. But it was also something that I knew I could not refuse to do. Somehow, by spilling as much beer down the front of my shirt as I dared, I managed to empty the stein and we collapsed into each other's arms.

That night Käthe asked us to do her a special favor. Their daughter Hanni had married an American GI and was now living on Henderson Avenue in the "Bron-ux," New York. Käthe wanted to send her a very special wedding gift. It was a glittering glass-eyed red fox whose sharp yellow teeth grasped the tip of its tail to form a lady's stole. It was so beautiful, Käthe said, and Hanni would love it so much, that she did not dare risk sending it through the post. Would we do her the very great favor of delivering it to Hanni personally? Of course we would.

We arrived in New York on a warm September day and collected our car, a little English Ford with immense aluminum license plates. My sons and I were all wearing Scottish travel caps. I got hopelessly lost in the Bronx trying to find Henderson Avenue. We had stopped at a long red light when a Bronx cab driver, with his window open, came alongside. I leaned over and asked one of my more inane questions. "I say," I said, "tell me, are we in the Bronx?" He looked slowly over the little car with its huge license plates and its capped occupants and mustachioed driver and said, "Well, I'll tell ya, Mac, it ain't Vassar."

He was quite right. When I laughed at my own stupidity, he smiled and said, "Whatsamattah? You lost or somethin'? Pull over to the side." I did and said, "I'm looking for 26 Henderson Avenue, the Bronx." After a long pause he said, "Henderson Avenue? . . . Yeah, Henderson Avenue . . . Now, that's very interestin'. Yeah, follow me, Mac." We followed him around several blocks and finally stopped in front of the apartment house where Hanni lived on a little street no more than three or four blocks long. I gave Geoff ten dollars and told him to thank the cab driver. He said, "Forget it, kid. Tell your father I've had a ball."

Let's get back to Germany. On days I did not go to the Institute in Munich, I went to the university, which was still in the process of reconstruction — some 70 percent had been destroyed during Allied bombing raids of 1943–1945. In February 1954 I attended lectures given by Professor Franz Schnabel (clad in heavy overcoat, muffler, and gray woolen gloves) to one hundred shivering students in an unheated lecture hall.

During the Nazi period, the University of Munich was the head-quarters of a resistance movement called the White Rose Society and led by a brother and sister, Hans and Sophie Scholl, supported by their professor of philosophy, Hans Huber. Sophie was caught dropping anti-Nazi leaflets down the great staircase in the university. A janitor turned her in to the Gestapo. After brutal torture that was unable to break her gallant spirit or force her to divulge names of fellow conspirators, she was beheaded on 18 February 1943.

Student memory is notoriously short-lived. But not student memory of Sophie Scholl. Every week fresh white roses appeared in a vase near the spot where she was arrested. And on the eleventh anniversary of her death, I attended a memorial service where hundreds of mourning students filled the great staircase and hall where she had dropped her leaflets. Students wept openly as they listened to a quartet playing Schubert's haunting *Death and the Maiden.*

The Scholls' memory is preserved in a more permanent way at the entrance to the university, where the little square is named *Geschwister-Scholl-Platz* (Brother and Sister Scholl Square.)

In a graduate seminar examining the differences between Americans and Germans, I was intrigued by an answer a student gave to a question. The professor had asked, "Well, Obermeyer, how would you define a German?" The student replied, "A German is someone who cannot admit that he is mistaken."

I took that extraordinary proposition under advisement and during the rest of my year in Germany I made it a point of seeing if the young man was right. I never did hear a German come flat out and say, "I was mistaken about that." Always there was some sort of circumlocution or explanation.

For instance: One evening we were chatting with the Thomamüllers, and Hans was saying that among the few good things about Hitler was his idea of the *Kraft durch Freude* (Strength through Joy) program that allowed workers to go on inexpensive vacations they could not otherwise afford. He recalled, "Ja, I really enjoyed my trip to Rome in August of 1937." Käthe commented, "I think it was in July, Hans." Hans replied,

"I said it was August." Käthe stuck to her guns: "It was July." Hans replied with some heat, "It was August, damn it!" Käthe quietly got up, went to the glass-doored *Schrank* in the parlor, and brought back to the kitchen table the postcard Hans had sent her from Rome. It was postmarked 18 July 1937. Hans looked at it and said, "*Ja,* typical! You never could trust those stupid Italian bureaucrats."

One of the indispensable tools of my trade is an inexpensive Scripto mechanical pencil with a large eraser. When I lost mine somewhere in Munich, I went into a large *Schreibwarengeschäft* to find a substitute. They had any number of school lead pencils with erasers. But not one of the mechanical pencils for grownups had an eraser.

THE THOMAMÜLLERS IN WILLIAMSTOWN

We had bid a warm farewell to the Thomamüllers in the summer of 1954, thinking that we might never see them again. We were mistaken. Some ten years later our phone rang in Williamstown, and I was surprised to hear the excited voice of Käthe calling from the neighboring town of Bennington, Vermont. She said that she and Hans had been visiting Hanni and her husband in the "Bron-ux," and they had come to visit us. She didn't know whether they could stay for a few days or maybe a week or two. They were in the bus depot; could I come up and get them? Of course I could.

They were delighted with the Green Mountains and the Berkshire hills, which reminded them of the foothills of their beloved Bavarian Alps. It had been pleasant seeing Hanni, but they really were not city people. They loved Williamstown and our house with its acre-sized yard. Käthe told us that they wanted to be put to work: particularly they wanted to work *"ins Freie"* — in the open air. Their garden at home in Ottobrunn was a showplace with many carefully edged flower beds, waterfalls, and little plaster Bavarian dwarfs fishing in the ponds, as well as many plaster birds and animals playing in the woods. Hans's left arm could be fitted with a hook, or a hammer, or a screwdriver. He could use a long-handled spade by running the handle through his hook and using it as a fulcrum. Käthe learned to operate the sit-down mower and Hans the edger, and in two days they had the lawn in better shape than it had ever been in its life. But they needed something else to do. They were not interested in American TV. They did not read at home, so were not interested in the German novels I brought them from the college library. They just wanted to work outdoors. During the next fortnight Anne and I would lie in bed at night, trying to think of things for them to do — preferably things that would take a good long time.

I had the bright idea of having them edge and level our long and winding gravel driveway with a covering of pea stone. I asked a contractor friend to bring us several yards. He said sure, and he would make my life easy by spreading it evenly and slowly from his dump truck. I urged him not to, explaining that it should take our guests a good long time to complete the job. They did it in less than two days. What next?

Hans had observed that we had a nice big yard, but it lacked one thing: a forest like the one he had at home. Didn't I know a forester who would give me some pine trees? I told him I was not at all sure I wanted a forest, but he was insistent, and since the forestation would, one hoped, take a good chunk of time, I acquiesced. I did actually know the man who was managing Hopkins Experimental Forest. He was amused by my problem and said he had a bunch of white pine seedlings he wanted thinned out. I borrowed a microbus and one afternoon we dug up fifty-six little trees. We unloaded them in the backyard and doused their roots in water. It was late afternoon and I thought we could wait till morning to plant them. No way. Hans and Käthe started right in. They broke for supper then set to work again. With the help of flashlights, they had all fifty-six planted by about ten o'clock that night. What next?

Hans wanted to build wooden bike racks for the boys' bicycles and asked me to supply him with some lumber. The college used an old barn for storing miscellaneous objects; outside the barn was a pile of used two-by-fours and other boards. The Director of Physical Plant said I could help myself. We went to the barn and chose enough lumber for several bike racks. Before leaving, Käthe looked in a dusty window and beckoned me to come over. She was looking longingly at a nearly life-size plaster statue of Joan of Arc seated and listening pensively to voices calling her from the forest. "Bob," she exclaimed, her eyes shining, "couldn't we take that for the front lawn?" I had discouraged her from decorating our lawn with dwarfs, fawns, and flamingos and I didn't think *Die Jungfrau von Orleans* would be an improvement. But Käthe was so desperately sincere, I had great difficulty dissuading her. I told her that we couldn't just take it, that it was probably being stored for the art department. She was not dissuaded. She pleaded with tears in her eyes. It was Friday afternoon, and they were leaving Williamstown the following Monday morning. It occurred to me that I might borrow the statue for the weekend. I called the Director of Physical Plant and told him my desperate plight and promised I would return the objet d'art no later than Monday afternoon. He said sure. I borrowed the microbus again and with two husky friends loaded and unloaded Joan. Käthe had wanted her sitting in the front yard, but I persuaded her that Joan would be much better under the pine trees in the back — better protected by the shade, for she was, after all, made of plaster. She agreed.

Sunday morning Anne and I went to church. We returned to find Joan mounted in concrete in which were embedded large rocks. She was glistening in the sun with two coats of bronze spray paint, which Hans had found, along with the instant cement, in my basement workshop. We were, quite literally, stuck with her.

Linz, Leonding, and Vienna

But let's go back a decade to my research in Germany. I had begun working on my Hitler study at the Institute in Munich. I also needed to go to Linz and the adjacent village of Leonding, as well as Vienna — places where Hitler had spent much of his boyhood and youth. We farmed out our two sons to friends at the American Consulate in Munich — reciprocity for having taken their two children while they spent a week in Paris — and looked forward to traveling on the *Orient Express* (Paris to Vienna to Istanbul), train of intrigue, mystery, and adventure. Anne, who was much taken with *The Lady Vanishes,* had visions of encountering tall, slinky femmes fatales smoking Turkish cigarettes from long holders and plotting international skulduggeries with Humphrey Bogart types in slouch hats and trench coats with turned-up collars and pockets bulging with automatic pistols. It was going to be a thrilling trip. Actually, it didn't turn out that way. The only other passenger in our coach was a lonely black GI playing plaintively on his mouth organ, "My momma done tol' me . . ."

Linz and Leonding were well worth the trip. In Leonding, I visited the elementary school and the little rococo Catholic church young Hitler had attended, the tavern where his brutal father had died of a heart attack, the graveyard where his mother and father were buried. Their pictures are on the tombstones erected not by the Führer but by the Nazi Party. Hitler did drop by briefly in 1937, to give the monuments a perfunctory glance, before turning on his heel and leaving. He never returned.

In Linz I walked the streets and saw the opera house that the pampered adolescent Adolf had visited in his silk shirt, opera cape, and ivory-handled walking stick. I found the Upper Austrian Provincial Archives particularly rewarding. The elderly archivist, Franz Jetzinger, had collected a great deal of material that he did not include in his book on Hitler's youth. Particularly, he very generously gave me copies of affidavits and transcripts of conversations he had had over the years with people who had known the Hitler family. He also gave me an affidavit from Hitler's only adolescent friend, his roommate in Vienna, August Kubizek. This statement differs importantly from Kubizek's published memoirs.

In Vienna I visited Stumpergasse 29, where young Hitler had rented a room from Frau Maria Zakreys that he shared with Kubizek and where, under a smoking paraffin lamp, he had tried to write a Wagnerian opera. In the Austrian National Library, I read dozens of tawdry anti-Semitic pamphlets — most notably a complete set of Lanz von Liebenfels's *Osteria* — the very pamphlets that Hitler had read and from which he had made what he called his "Copernican Discovery" that all history is determined by blood.

Wald Trudering: "Sitting-Down Facilities" and an Erased Swastika

Three years later I enjoyed another sabbatical leave in Germany that we spent in the suburban village of Wald Trudering. Here we rented an apartment over the Beelers. Herr Beeler worked in the Ministry of Culture and graciously supplied us with inexpensive tickets to concerts and the opera. Frau Beeler was a good-humored and attractively sturdy farm girl who was heavily pregnant. She took twenty-four hours off from her daily toil to give birth to a healthy boy. Anne helped with the postnatal care and both of our sons held the baby when he was a few hours old. We were godparents at his midwinter baptism, during which the squalling baby was totally unwrapped and sprinkled with holy water in the ice-cold stone village church.

On Saturdays Peter borrowed Frau Beeler's old one-speed woman's bicycle to cycle through the woods to visit his old friends the Thomamüllers in Ottobrunn.

Heinrich Himmler of the SS had had a chicken farm in Wald Trudering and the village elementary school Geoffrey and Peter would attend had had its former name, Heinrich Himmler Volkschule, and swastika insignia blasted off its gateway. The day before school was to open, I walked through the woods to the school to register the boys for the year. In the schoolyard I asked a little girl the director's name. She told me and said that his office was on the third floor. I introduced myself to Herr Oberlehrer Schmidt and asked if I could register my sons. He surprised me by asking, "What is your religion?" When I told him I was Protestant, he said, "Then it is impossible. Your sons cannot attend my school." I told him my understanding was that this was the general elementary school for the village and that a little girl had told me that he was the director. He replied, "Oh. She was no doubt a Catholic girl. You must understand that we have, in effect, three schools in one building. On the top floor here, we have Catholic girls; below us are the Catholic boys; and on the bottom, the Protestants. That is where you should go and speak with Herr Neumeyer."

I thanked him and congratulated him on his careful organization in terms of the likelihood of ultimate salvation, with little Catholic girls closest to heaven, the Protestant boys far below. He was not at all amused; indeed, he became quite flustered and said, "No, no, it is not at all a question of spiritual salvation; it is simply a matter of sanitation. The top floor is where we have the *Sitzengelegenheiten* (sitting-down facilities)."

The boys separated when Peter followed his friend to the Catholic school and Geoffrey went to the Protestant school. We realized this when Geoffrey came home on Luther's birthday with a commemorative picture of the great man. Peter thought he had been shortchanged, complaining that they didn't give out pictures of Martin Luther in his school — in fact, they never even mentioned him. Since he liked his teacher and got on well with the kids, we let him stay Catholic for the rest of the year.

During this autumn of 1959 there had been an ominous resurgence of neo-Nazism in Munich. Jewish cemeteries had once more been defaced and the swastika appeared on walls and buildings. Peter's teacher, Herr Neumeyer, invited me to visit his class in history to hear him discuss the *Hitlerzeit*. That was not an easy topic for him, since he himself had been a member of the SA (*Sturm Abteilungen,* the Brown Shirts) and many of the pupils' fathers, uncles, and grandfathers had been supporters of Hitler. His performance was courageous and effective.

Neumeyer started the class by saying that he had been a member of the SA, and now deeply regretted it. Then he described the concentration-camp system. He read harrowing passages from prisoners' diaries and memoirs. The class was transfixed. Then he asked, "What is the swastika?" There was a long, uneasy silence and then a boy said, "That's a sign people paint on walls." Neumeyer's face blanched and his voice trembled with emotion as he repeated what the boy had said: "A sign people paint on walls, eh?"

With half a piece of chalk held flat in his hand, he drew a broad swastika on the blackboard. Then he said, "Let me tell you something, children, and I hope you'll never forget what I tell you now. The swastika was once an ancient sign of life and hope and purity. A good sign. Under Hitler it became a sign of cruelty, filth, hatred, and death. No decent person will ever paint that sign on a wall again. *Never!* We must wipe it out." And he swept it from the board.

Let's change the subject and backtrack a little. Shortly after we arrived in Munich, like virtually everyone else, Anne and I visited the famous tavern of the *Hofbräuhaus* (royal brewery). I was particularly attracted to the enormous hall called the *Schweme* (horse trough; hence, watering place). Here, we were told, 5,000 people can be watered with one-liter steins of beer brought by generously proportioned waitresses, as many as eight steins held in one hand, while an oompah band in lederhosen plays Munich drinking songs. The *Schweme* is a favorite luncheon spot for farmers who have brought their produce to the nearby open market. Typically, they and their wives order a *Masskrog* of beer each, open a satchel and remove home-baked bread and a huge white radish, and then proceed with their lunch. Radish and beer are such a familiar combination in Munich that the religious logo of the city, a haloed *Münchener Kindl,* depicting a little monk *(Münchin)* with a crucifix in one hand and a prayer book in the other, is replaced in souvenir stores by the same monk with a stein of beer in one hand, a white radish in the other.

On our first visit for lunch I tried to decipher the extremely long and complex bill of fare. Since Anne was fond of veal, I ordered something I thought she would like. It took a very long time coming. Finally, she was served her meal: one entire calf's head, jellied, with green grapes stuck in its eye sockets. Anne gamely scraped a morsel or two from the calf's jowl and then gave up. When I asked her if she would like me to get her a doggie bag, she replied, somewhat coolly, "No, thank you. And from now on I'll order my own meals."

LENIN, HITLER, AND THE *HOFBRÄUHAUS*

While doing research at the *Institut für Zeitgeschichte* in Munich, I came across a story that links Vladimir I. Lenin with the *Hofbräuhaus* and, indirectly, with Adolf Hitler.

A quirk of fate had brought both men to Munich, where both had lived in Schwabing in the Schleissheimerstrasse. A dozen years before Hitler arrived, Lenin had rented a room above a cabinetmaker, just up the street from Popp's tailor shop, where Hitler would live. There, in 1902, Lenin had written the most influential political pamphlet of the twentieth century, *What Is to Be Done?* In it he inverted Marx and argued that in revolutionary action, politics took priority over economics. He set forth in clear and specific prose how a political elite of professional revolutionaries could seize power and determine the economic and social structure of a country and the world.

Both Lenin and Hitler had bought their bread at Herr Heilmann's bakery; Lenin, too, had eaten meals in Hitler's favorite restaurant, the Osteria Bavaria, and had drunk beer at the *Hofbräuhaus,* the scene of Hitler's early party triumphs.

In 1960 I had a conversation with a very old but still spry little man who had been Lenin's landlord, the cabinetmaker in the Schleissheimerstrasse. He told me that his famous tenant had always been neatly dressed, polite, kind to children in the block, gallant to the ladies, and prompt with his rent. He worked hard and seldom took time off to relax. One Saturday evening, however, he and Krupskaya, his wife, joined the landlord and his wife for a convivial evening in the *Hofbräuhaus*. Lenin kept laughing and nudging his wife as they all linked arms and sang the old drinking song "*In München stet 'n Hofbräuhaus*" while raising their liter steins decorated with the crown of Bavaria and the initials HB. But Lenin was not toasting the royal brewery that evening. He was drinking to a very different HB. Those letters in the Russian alphabet are NV. And that, to Lenin, stood for *Narodnaya Volya,* the revolutionary "Will of the People."

Here, in the *Hofbräuhaus,* Lenin was giving a graphic illustration of Axelrod's comment that the reason Lenin excelled all other Russian revolutionaries was this: "He is the only one of us who works at revolution twenty-four hours a day: the twenty hours he's awake and the four hours he is sleeping, when he dreams of revolution."

That includes, one may add, a couple of hours he spent drinking beer.

Ainmillerstrasse, Hitler's Seat, and "The Wild Chase"

For our next sabbatical in Munich, in 1967, Anne suggested that we live in the city itself. She had enjoyed village life, but she thought it would be fun to live in Schwabing, the Left Bank area of the city near the university. Both boys were in school — Geoffrey at Harvard, concentrating in German, and Peter at Repton School in Derbyshire, concentrating in art. Since considerable new building had taken place since 1953, we were able to rent a furnished modern studio apartment in the Ainmillerstrasse, just off the Leopoldstrasse and north of the Siegestor, the arch that marks the entrance to the university. This triumphal arch was designed by King Ludwig I as a monument to the Bavarian army. Badly damaged in a 1944 bombing raid, it was only partially restored, leaving the scars of war and a new inscription on its southern side: *Dem Sieg geweiht, im Krieg zerstört, zum Friede mahnend* (Dedicated to victory, destroyed in war, an admonition to peace).

While living in Ainmillerstrasse, I enjoyed walking the streets that Hitler had walked in 1914. I visited 106 Schleissheimerstrasse, where he had lived above the tailor shop of Josef Popp. His room was pleasant, comfortably furnished, and had a private entrance from the street. Hitler could have invited either female or male guests to his room. The Popps had no objections. Yet, as they recalled with some surprise, Hitler never invited anyone. Popp had been trained in Paris and prided himself on being a master tailor of modish fashions. Since he was a kindly man and also one who did not wish his tenants' clothing to cast aspersions on his business, he supplied Hitler with well-cut suits and an overcoat. The

Popp children, young "Jupp" and Elisabeth, liked the nice man who lived upstairs. Yet, as they said in an interview, "He never talked about his own family and we never could find out what he was really like."

Hitler was also befriended by a kindly baker just around the corner, at Gabelsbergerstrasse 66, who sold him day-old rolls for a few pennies. This baker, Herr Heilmann, said in an interview that "Hitler never did any manual work" and always appeared clean and neatly dressed. The baker also said that Hitler sold his paintings for ten to twenty-five marks each and that he himself had purchased two.

After he sold a painting, Hitler liked to take a meal at the Osteria Bavaria restaurant. An elderly waitress pointed out to me the chair in which he invariably sat, in a corner, with his back to the wall. I had the dubious privilege of sitting in "the Führer's chair."

During their summer holidays, Geoffrey and Peter visited us, and one day, after seeing some of the many art galleries of the city, Geoff burst into our flat on the Ainmillerstrasse and said, "Dad, did you know that there's a portrait of Adolf Hitler in the Municipal Gallery at the Lenbachhaus?" With that total confidence of superior knowledge that comes with parenthood and does so much to bridge the generation gap, I replied with condescension, "No, son, there is no Hitler portrait in the Municipal Gallery. Local officials simply would not permit it." Whereupon Peter piped up, "But there is, Dad, and he's riding on a horse."

"That clinches it," I responded. "Hitler was terrified by horses. He enjoyed looking at statues of stallions, but he certainly would never have ridden one." Geoff responded sensibly, "Will you at least come and *look?*"

The next day we went to look. And the boys appeared to be right. There seemed to be a portrait of Adolf Hitler under the title of *Die wilde Jagd* (Wild or Mad Chase). In this terrifying picture, the artist has caught the spirit of the Teutonic legend of Wotan, the mad hunter, personification of death and destruction, who rides forth at night leaving horror in his wake. This Wotan bears an uncanny likeness to the Führer. Here is the same dark brown hair with the famous forelock over the left temple, the piercing eyes, the large nose, the Charlie Chaplin mustache.

Hitler's favorite images are also pictured: decapitation, wolves, and death. At the tip of the mad huntsman's sword dangles a human head; wolflike animals howl at the horse; hollow-eyed little creatures yell soundlessly; and ravished women and corpses are left in the path of the galloping horseman.

But to the student of Hitler, the single fact that sent chills up my spine that summer day — the most arresting thing about this apotheosis of rampaging destruction that directly associates Hitler with the mad Wotan — was the inscription in the lower left-hand corner of the painting. It reads: *"Franz Stuck, Mein erstes Olgemälde, 1889."*

Adolf Hitler was born on 20 April 1889.

Japanese Flip-flops in Prague

We told the boys that while they were on holiday they could visit the city of their choice. Peter chose Berlin because he wanted to see the East German guards and go through Checkpoint Charlie, which he had seen in adventure movies. Since Geoff had written an honors essay on Kafka, he chose to visit Prague. He particularly wanted to see where Kafka had lived and to pay respects at his grave.

Our drive across East Germany to Berlin and back was relatively uneventful. Prague was more interesting. We were obliged to make all travel arrangements through Čedok, the government travel office, which reserved for the three of us a luxurious suite of rooms in a mansion that had obviously been commandeered by the Communist government. The staid ambience was made lively by the arrival of delegates from all Warsaw Pact countries, who had arrived for some sort of Communist powwow.

We visited the Kafka house in the alley by the castle, with its famous "defenestration" window, and then sought Kafka's grave. Foolishly thinking it would be in the old Jewish Cemetery, we found that that had been closed to further burials since the eighteenth century. During the Nazi occupation the old burial ground was called "the saddest place on earth." Here the SS permitted Jewish children to play among the ancient stones of their ancestors before they were shipped off to their own deaths. The whitewashed walls and flat dome of the old adjacent synagogue were rendered gray by the carefully inscribed names of thousands upon thousands of Jews who were murdered by the Nazis. For Franz Kafka's grave, we were advised to go to the "New Jewish Cemetery."

We finally found it in the late August afternoon. The iron gate was off its hinges, and the cemetery was a tangle of weeds, brambles and underbrush. The chances of finding Kafka's grave were minimal, but Geoffrey was determined. We wandered around ineffectively till finally an elderly woman dressed in black approached and asked if she could be helpful. I said we sought the grave of Dr. Franz Kafka. She looked surprised and her face brightened. She said in German, "Oh, then I can help you. I am Franz Kafka's niece." She walked with us to a well-cared-for grave. I thanked her warmly and then asked a mindless question: "Isn't it a shame that the other graves have been rather neglected?" Her quiet reply was unforgettable: "Who is left to care?"

One or two places away from where Franz Kafka lies, there is a grave marked AVRAM HIEDLER. That is the spelling Adolf Hitler's relatives had sometimes used.

When we returned late that evening to our hotel, I noticed a sign inside the outer door of our suite that invited honored guests who wished to have shoes shined to place them in the hallway at night. We were assured, in three languages, that the shoes would be shined and returned early the following morning. I travel light. I had packed one pair of Japanese flip-flops and wore a pair of heavy cordovan brogues that were getting a bit scuffy. I told Anne I was going to take advantage of their service. Her advice was clear: "Don't do it! Those are good shoes. You'll never see them again. Just don't do it." I scorned her advice.

The next morning I asked her to come to the door with me so that I could show her how mistaken she was. She accompanied me to the door. I opened it and arrested my sweeping gesture in midair. No shoes.

Furious, I got fully dressed, wearing my old flip-flops. I tried unsuccessfully to look irate and dignified as I flip-flopped noisily down the broad marble steps to the reception desk. I reported the theft to the clerk. He said it couldn't possibly be a theft. They didn't have thefts. It was no doubt a "little joke" one of my comrades, probably from Poland, was playing on me. I said it was no joke and if I didn't have my shoes returned in fifteen minutes, "You, Comrade, are going to be in trouble.

Serious trouble." I turned sharply on my rubbery heels and flip-flopped back up the stairs. I had not specified the kind of trouble in store for him, because I hadn't the foggiest idea what it might be, but no matter. In ten minutes the shoes were returned with a large orange placed in each heel.

We packed; I put in a call for our car to be delivered to the front door. We went downstairs and as Anne and Geoff waited in the foyer, I stood outside under the canopy waiting for our car. I was dressed in a blue blazer, white shirt and predominantly red rep-striped tie, and nicely shined cordovan shoes. A Brunhilde-sized blonde from East Germany rushed up to me, gave me a bear hug of major proportions and said, "Comrade, you run an excellent hotel! Excellent! For you I am going to write a strong letter of commendation."

I thanked her, smiled and said, "Comrade, we can only do our best!"

IN SEARCH OF ADOLF HITLER

My interest in Adolf Hitler began in Benson High School. I wrote a weekly column for our school newspaper, *The Gopher's Whistle,* devoted to contemporary news: "Around the World with Bob Waite" — a remarkably pretentious title for a fifteen-year-old columnist who had never traveled beyond Manitoba and Minnesota.

During the 1930s the news that captured the attention of our generation was the amazing rise to power of the Führer. The questions I asked as a high school student were the same questions I would ask as a professional historian: How was it possible that the culture that gave us great names in music, literature, medicine, science, and the arts could embrace a government that was in very truth "the negation of God erected into a system of governance"? How could the German people hail as their savior this peculiar little man, this mentally flawed failure, this psychopath?

I was particularly intrigued by the voice we heard at night saying, "This is William L. Shirer calling from Berlin." His ingenuity in bypassing Nazi censorship, and the very fact that we knew he could not tell the whole story of life in the Third Reich, or what Hitler was really like, only whetted my appetite for more knowledge and a fuller answer to that historical question that is at once the most simple and the most sophisticated a historian can ask: *Why?* Why Hitler?

VANGUARD OF NAZISM:
The German Free Corps Movement

In college and graduate school I discovered that there were many, many pieces to that complex puzzle of why Hitler came to power. I found one piece in my research for the doctorate: It was the Free Corps Movement of 1919–1923. These were volunteer formations of battle-tough German soldiers who were dismayed, as one of them said, "when peace broke out." The new republican government made the nearly catastrophic decision of hiring these men to protect it from the perceived threat of socialist takeover.

Meanwhile, one day in the late summer of 1919, Adolf Hitler raised his strangely compelling voice in a back room of a Munich tavern to demand that the dozen men who formed the "German Workers' Party" purchase a single rubber stamp to improve their office equipment.

That same summer the *Freikorps* (Free Corps) had become the most important political force in Germany. A million men strong, they were sweeping the country with a doctrine that differed in no essential way from future Nazism. They formed, I concluded in my first book, the *Vanguard of Nazism* (Harvard University Press, 1953). Reichsmarschall Hermann Göring would have agreed with the title. He later hailed them as "the first soldiers of the Third Reich."

Their contribution to Hitler was twofold: first, a negative one. Politically, the Weimar Republic was, indeed, as one of its chancellors said in a brilliant metaphor, "a candle burning at both ends." The Free Corps and their successor organizations saw to it that the flame on the Right end of the candle burned more brightly and melted more wax than its competitor on the Left.

They also made specific positive contributions to Hitler. In droves, "Free Corps fighters" rose to positions of influence and power in Hitler's Reich. They contributed a well-developed *Führerprinzip,* youth groups, labor camps, racial theory, vicious anti-Semitism, and the mystic adoration of what they called the *"Volk* soul."

But the real importance of the *Freikorps* lies in none of these things. It lies, I concluded, "in that brutality of spirit, in that exaltation of power which the men of the Free Corps bequeathed to the Third Reich."

Yet my study of the Free Corps didn't respond to my question about the personality of Adolf Hitler. What was it about him that attracted these soldiers by the thousands? There were a dozen heroic military personalities in postwar Germany who would seem more appealing to these tough veterans than this noisy political rabble-rouser. Obviously, they found something compelling about his personality, but what was it?

"Dr. Sedgwick," Dan McGrew, and Putzi Hanfstaengl

Help with that answer came one afternoon in a telephone call to my office on the top floor of Stetson Library at Williams. My colleague James MacGregor Burns, who was in Hyde Park Library working on what would be his Pulitzer Prize-winning biography of Franklin D. Roosevelt, said he had just come across a document that might interest me. It was a typescript entitled "Adolf Hitler" and dated December 1942. Across the title page was written: "File FDR Personal, Confidential." Jim went on to say that the manuscript seemed to contain intimate details of Hitler's personal life, attitudes, and habits, and asked if I would like him to send me a photocopy. I would indeed.

The sixty-eight-page manuscript was full of fascinating information about Hitler's personality. Much of it depended on the testimony of someone who knew the Führer intimately, a certain "Dr. Sedgwick." I had never heard of him. Who was this mysterious person?

Only three people knew Hitler that well: his *"du-Freund"* Ernst Röhm — but Hitler had had him shot in 1934 during the "Blood Purge"; Rudolph Hess, Hitler's fellow prisoner in Landsberg Fortress — but in 1942 Hess was in the Tower of London after his ill-fated flight to Scotland; and Ernst "Putzi" Hanfstaengl, the scion of a famous Munich family who often entertained Hitler in the Hanfstaengl villa. Putzi was the likely candidate. But why "Dr. Sedgwick"?

The official *Deutsche Führerlexikon* (a sort of Who's Who of the Nazi Party) answered my question. Putzi's full name was Ernst Franz Sedgwick Hanfstaengl. His grandmother was a Sedgwick, a distinguished New

England family, two of whose members had been Union generals in the Civil War. In their burial plot in the town of Stockbridge, Massachusetts, family members are buried in a circle with their feet together. When they arise in the Great Hereafter, Sedgwicks prefer to be greeted by Sedgwicks.

Putzi's grandfather Franz had established the Hanfstaengl Art Publishing Company and made the family fortune by developing a photographic technique that reproduced oil paintings with great fidelity. Putzi graduated from Harvard College in 1910. He was a fellow alumnus along with Franklin Roosevelt and, like him, a member of the Hasty Pudding Club, and both men had taken History 1, a famous introductory course in European history. A gifted musician, Putzi was an active member of the Harvard marching band; he also rowed on the Harvard eight. After doing graduate work in England, France, Italy, and Austria, he took his Ph.D. in history at the University of Munich.

In 1922, he met Adolf Hitler and was captivated. Putzi was a considerable asset to Hitler and his struggling party. His name provided social respectability, and his knowledge of art and music and his bumptious good humor appealed to the rising political agitator. Early in 1923 Hanfstaengl provided funds for the purchase of the *Völkischer Beobachter,* the party newspaper that was indispensable to Hitler's success. Because of Putzi's fluency in four languages and his international connections, Hitler made him Chief of Foreign Press for the Nazi Party.

Putzi and his wife, Hélene, often entertained the Führer in their spacious home in the fashionable Bogenhausen section of Munich. Putzi was a powerful pianist, and after an emotionally draining speech, Hitler would relax in the Hanfstaengl living room as Putzi banged out Wagner on his concert-size Bechstein.

After the failure of Hitler's Beer Hall Putsch in November 1923, Hitler ran away and hid in the Hanfstaengls' summer home on Staffel Lake, some thirty miles southwest of Munich. There, when in a fit of despondency Hitler tried to shoot himself, Mrs. Hanfstaengl seized his revolver and threw it into a barrel of flour she was hoarding.

Arrested and confined to comfortable quarters in Landsberg prison, he dictated *Mein Kampf,* the book that would make him famous and wealthy. He served only seven months of a five-year sentence and was released before Christmas 1924. His first stop on returning to Munich was the Hanfstaengls' home. He appeared at their door and told Putzi to play Wagner's "Liebestod" for him.

Shortly after the Second World War began, Putzi was captured by the British and sent to a prisoner-of-war camp in Canada. There he persuaded a Hearst correspondent visiting the camp to deliver a letter he had written to President Franklin Roosevelt, his fellow Harvardian, offering his services as a political advisor in the fight against Hitler. The president accepted his proposal. While technically remaining in British custody, Putzi was lent out to the American government. He was taken to a stately home in Virginia and there, using the name "Dr. Sedgwick," he wrote the description of Hitler that would be used in the manuscript Jim Burns sent me from the Hyde Park Library.

I knew that I could gain a great deal from interviewing Putzi Hanfstaengl. In 1967, when I was making plans for my sabbatical in Munich, I learned that he was still living in the family home in the city. But I was told that he had become very much of a recluse and would not grant interviews. During the war he had not been received in the States as cordially as he had expected. He was particularly bitter that his fellow alumnus Franklin Roosevelt had shown little inclination to cozy up to him. The U.S. Government was interested only in pumping him for information, and he was fed up with telling people everything he knew about the Führer.

It would be extremely difficult to get an interview with Hanfstaengl, but it was worth a shot. I wrote him a letter and hoped the salutation would catch his attention: "Dear Dr. Sedgwick." I knew he was sentimental about his years at Harvard, so I played the Harvard card by saying how honored I had been to teach in his History 1, that course he and Frank Roosevelt had both enjoyed. I also expressed the pleasure I had had in having his attractive son Egon in class. (Egon really was a fine young man and an excellent student.) I said I was coming to Munich and that I would look forward very much to meeting him. I ended by asking if I might ring him when I arrived.

Shortly after we were settled in the Ainmillerstrasse flat, I found his address and unlisted telephone number through the *Institut für Zeitgeschichte*. Our telephone conversation follows:

> *I:* Robert Waite here. May I speak to Dr. Sedgwick?
>
> *He:* (after a long pause) Where were you born?
>
> *I:* I was born in Canada.
>
> *He:* Canada, eh? Who was Robert W. Service?
>
> *I:* "A bunch of the boys were whooping it up in the Malamute Saloon; The kid that handles the music box was hitting a jag-time tune . . ."
>
> *He:* Come and see me! Tomorrow at noon.
>
> *I:* Thank you. I look forward to that.

When I knocked at the door of the Hanfstaengl villa, Pienzenauerstrasse, 52 in the Bogenhausen, a panel slid back, revealing an iron-grid window about seven inches square. From behind the grid a voice said, "'There stumbled a miner fresh from the creeks, dog-dirty and loaded for bear.'" It then stopped.

It was my turn to finish the verse: "'He looked like a man with a foot in the grave and scarcely the strength of a louse, / Yet he tilted a poke of dust on the bar, and he called for drinks for the house.'"

I heard heavy bars being slid back, the massive oak door opened and the voice said, "Come in!" I had passed the test.

Before me stood a slightly stooped giant of some six feet, five inches, and 260 rather flabby pounds. "Putzi" in Bavarian means tiny. Hanfstaengl was tiny the way Robin Hood's Little John was little.

First he plied me with questions about my childhood in Canada, never telling me that he had spent time there as a British prisoner. He invited me to take lunch with him. Lunch consisted — as it would every day I visited him — of Mosel wine and gingersnaps. In the future I supplied the Mosel and he the gingersnaps sent to him in huge quantities from London.

He showed me how he had seated the leaders of the Nazi movement around the large living room and indicated the chairs where they had sat on a typical social evening. Then he described their personalities, strengths and weaknesses, and their conversations. He let me hold, like a holy relic, the English travel rug Hitler had used when he fled to his summer home after the putsch; his ham-size hands hammered out Hitler's favorite tunes on the Bechstein.

On one occasion he asked, "Now, Professor Waite, would you like to know Harvard's gift to the Third Reich?" I said that I would. Well, one evening, he said, he had amused the Führer by playing American football rousers: "Cheer, cheer for old Notre Dame . . . On, Wisconsin; on, Wisconsin . . . Minnesota, hats off to thee."

"In the middle of a rousing version of the Harvard Fight Song, 'Hah-vuhd, Hah-vhud, Fight!' Hitler jumped up, grabbed me by the shoulders and shouted enthusiastically, 'Hanfstaengl! Hanfstaengl! That's it! That's what we need for our movement: *Sieg Heil! Sieg Heil! Sieg Heil!*' You see, Waite, that was Harvard's gift to the Third Reich."

Ernst Hanfstaengl was not an appealing luncheon host. He seated me at his side on a well-worn sofa. While he ate gingersnaps with one hand, he held in the other a water tumbler about a quarter full of sputum. He had a chronic catarrhal condition that caused him to hawk up phlegm loudly and spit it sloppily into the water glass.

Someplace in the voluminous so-called *Tischgespräche* that records the Führer's midnight soliloquies in his air-raid shelter during the war, Hitler makes a statement that I can verify from personal experience. He says, "You know, Hanfstaengl was stingy."

He was, indeed. As we were eating lunch side by side one day, I happened to drop a small piece of slightly moist gingersnap onto the very dirty Oriental rug. I picked it up and dropped it into a wastebasket. Without interrupting his stream of words, Putzi reached into the basket, retrieved the half-eaten biscuit and put it into his mouth.

I had gained a very great deal from my week's conversations with Hanfstaengl. But I knew our meetings had to terminate. There are limits beyond which I will not go for the sake of historical research. One of those limits was exceeded when, during a conversation, he started to rub the palm of his huge hand up and down my inner thigh. Another was

Harvard's gift to the Third Reich

his response to what would be my last question. The conversation had gone like this:

I: Dr. Hanfstaengl, you are a student of history, and have written a book on European political leaders. In looking back over Hitler's career, how would you evaluate him as a statesman?

He: I'd say he was about 90 percent right.

I: Oh, that's a very high percentage for any statesman. Where did he go wrong?

He: Barbarossa! We never should have invaded Soviet Russia. Big mistake, big mistake.

I: And the Jews, what about the Jews?

He: Oh, ya, the Jews. You know, we got so many of the wrong ones.

I got up and left the room.

THE OSS FILE ON HITLER

The more I learned about Adolf Hitler, the more I realized that the man was mentally disturbed. I needed psychopathic help. When I talked about this dimension of the "Hitler Problem" to my colleagues at the Institute, they said they had heard that during the war, agents of the OSS (the predecessor of the CIA) had collected a great deal of "psychological stuff" under the general code name "Operation Ashcan" and that it was now in the files of the CIA. When I returned to Williamstown, I wrote a letter to Richard Helms, then director of the CIA.

After graduating from Williams College in 1935 with a major in history, Helms worked for a time as a journalist in Germany and became greatly interested in Hitler. In my letter to him I described my project on Hitler and asked him if a former OSS file on Hitler existed in the CIA and, if so, would I be able to see it? I also told him what a pleasure it was to have his son Dennis in my class in German history. He responded with a friendly and helpful letter, saying that such material did indeed exist, but unfortunately it was classified. He saw no reason, however, not to declassify it and make it available to me. He invited me to look him up when I went to Washington to read the material. I wrote back thanking him for his courtesy but saying we were in the middle of exams at Williams and I couldn't easily get away. Would it be possible to have all the material copied at my expense and sent to me? Within a week I received a large parcel containing three thick mimeographed volumes labeled "OSS Source Book" and one volume entitled "A Psychological Analysis of Adolph [sic] Hitler: His Life and Legend," by

Walter C. Langer, with the collaboration of Henry A. Murray, Harvard Psychological Clinic; Ernst Kris, New School for Social Research; and Bertram D. Lewin, New York Psychoanalytic Institute. No date was given, but it was probably 1943. (In 1972 Basic Books published a revised version of this analysis, *The Mind of Adolf Hitler: The Secret Wartime Report,* Foreword by William L. Langer, Afterword by Robert G. L. Waite.)

The thin manuscript Jim Burns had sent me from the Hyde Park Library that set me on the trail of Putzi Hanfstaengl turned out to be a brief preliminary statement of a much larger project suggested by President Roosevelt. During the war, he had wanted to know his enemy. Realizing that Adolf Hitler was psychologically disturbed, FDR sought to find out the nature of his pathology to determine what actions Hitler might take. The president ordered "Wild Bill" Donovan, the head of the OSS, to find out. Donovan consulted with William L. Langer, the distinguished Harvard University professor of European history, who was currently serving as head of the historical section of the OSS. They directed OSS agents, at home and abroad, to interview dozens of people —- of whom Hanfstaengl was one — who had known Hitler. Hundreds of affidavits were collected for the three-volume OSS Source Books. Professor Langer then asked his brother Walter, a well-known psychoanalyst, to study this raw material and write a psychological analysis of Hitler's personality. Some five copies of this "secret wartime report" were printed in 1943. They went to Roosevelt, Churchill, and, I believe, three Allied generals.

Langer's prediction about Hitler's last days was uncannily prescient. Written in the autumn of 1943, it is an accurate description of what actually happened in the spring of 1945:

> *Whatever else happens, we may be reasonably sure that as Germany suffers successive defeats Hitler will become more and more neurotic. Each defeat will shake his confidence still further and limit his opportunities for proving his own greatness to himself. In consequence he will feel himself more and more vulnerable to attack from his associates and*

his rages will increase in frequency. He will probably try to compensate for his vulnerability by stressing his brutality and ruthlessness.

As I commented in my Afterword, Hitler had, indeed, always imagined himself to be a totally masculine, infallible, and brutal leader whose ideal for German youth expressed his own self-idealization: "Youth must be lithe and taut, swift as greyhounds, tough as leather and hard as Krupp steel." But now, in the spring of 1945, it was increasingly apparent that the soft-muscled, paunchy man with the shuffling gait, gray skin, and trembling effeminate hands did not at all fit his own picture of the all-conquering Führer. Each military defeat unnerved him further and required more proof that he was the ice-cold, steel-hard, brutal victor of his fantasies. Since he could not play that role by conquering either the Soviet Union or the Western Allies, he now manufactured "victory" over what he termed "my greatest enemy, the Jew." He conquered his unarmed and helpless enemy in gas chambers.

While destroying the "Jewish Peril," he sought also to destroy the Germany that, he yelled in a voice cracking with fury, was no longer worthy of him. Everything was to be smashed — everything essential to life: not only industrial plants but water, gas, and electrical works; ration-card files, records of birth, marriage, and death; bank accounts, hospitals, farms. Woodlands were to be burned, cattle slaughtered. Works of art, museums, monuments, cathedrals, opera houses — everything Hitler had once loved — were to be utterly destroyed.

The idea is conveyed clearly in an editorial that, at the Führer's express command, appeared in one of the last issues of the party organ, *Völkischer Beobachter:* "Not a German shock of wheat is to feed the enemy, not a German mouth to give him information, not a German hand to offer him help. He is to find nothing but death, annihilation and hatred."

Used with caution, I found material in the OSS Source Books helpful, and the analysis of Hitler by Walter Langer suggestive. But I still sought the advice of other psychoanalysts. Fortunately for me, Erik H. Erikson was in residence at the Riggs Clinic in Stockbridge, just thirty miles from Williamstown. He had long been interested in Hitler and had written a penetrating early essay on Hitler's childhood based on a psychological analysis of *Mein Kampf*. Erikson was remarkably generous with his time and kindly read several chapters of the manuscript for my first Hitler book.

W. H. Auden's Contribution

Exceedingly helpful, too, was Norbert Bromberg, M.D., then retired Clinical Professor of Psychiatry at Albert Einstein College of Medicine. We had many hours of fruitful conversations in each other's homes, and Dr. Bromberg contributed the title for my Hitler biography by recommending that I read a poem written by W. H. Auden.

Auden had lived in Germany and Austria and was a warm admirer of German literature and music. He was also impressed with Sigmund Freud's insights into the human psyche. Like all civilized people, he was appalled by Hitler. When the *Wehrmacht* smashed into Poland on 1 September 1939, unleashing the Second World War, Auden was in a bar in New York. Deeply depressed by the brutal attack on all he held dear, he ordered a martini and started to write the poem he titled "1 September 1939."

In an effort to come to grips with Adolf Hitler, I was attempting to combine the insights of both historical analysis and psychology. In one verse of this poem Auden was challenging me to do exactly that:

> *Accurate scholarship can unearth the whole offense*
> *From Luther until now that has driven a culture mad.*
> *Find out what occurred in Linz,*
> *What huge Imago made a psychopathic god.*
> *I and the public know what all schoolchildren learn*
> *Those to whom evil is done, do evil in return.*

Auden had given me the title for my book: *Psychopathic God: Adolf Hitler.* Now I needed to get his permission to use it and to print the verse on the frontispiece of the book. But getting that permission was more difficult than I had imagined. I knew that Auden at that time was a Fellow of All Souls' College, Oxford. I wrote to him there, saying I was trying to do what he told me to do in that verse. I got no reply. I contacted his New York agent, who was sympathetic but said that Mr. Auden no longer liked that poem and refused to have it anthologized. I said I appreciated Auden's feelings but I did not want the entire poem, only that one verse, which expressed in poetic form exactly what I was attempting in my study of Hitler — that immense phenomenon we both were trying to comprehend. After several weeks of waiting, I received word that Auden approved.

KLAUS RICHTER CONTRIBUTES A COVER

I had a title for my book; now I needed a cover. Since there were literally hundreds of studies of Adolf Hitler, I wanted a really striking picture. It had to depict a psychopathic god. And that would not be easy to find.

One afternoon as I sat working in the *Institut für Zeitgeschichte,* a German graduate student I had met at the university came to me and asked if I had seen a portrait of Hitler in Bad Godesberg. I said I had not. He responded with considerable intensity, "But you must! You must! It's *strange,* really *strange!" (Seltsam ist es! Wirklich seltsam!)*

The next week, Anne and I drove to Bad Godesberg and found the Luder Niemeyer gallery. Both of us stood transfixed before the portrait of Adolf Hitler. It was indeed, and at the very least, strange. I really don't know how to describe this compelling, this mad portrayal of the Führer. The artist was Klaus Richter (1887–1948), a noted painter who was professor of portraiture at the Berlin Academy. He had done portraits of Field Marshal von Schlieffen and Chancellor Stressmann, among many others.

Richter's widow explained the unusual circumstances under which this Hitler portrait had been produced. Early in 1941 Reichsmarschall Hermann Göring had "invited" Richter to Karinhalle, his palatial home, to do his portrait. During one of the sittings Richter remarked that the Führer had never had his portrait painted from life — his annual official portraits were all painted from photographs. Hitler would never sit still long enough to be painted. Göring was pleased with how his own portrait was going and felt in an expansive mood. Enjoying his propensity for throwing his very considerable weight around, he said he might be able to arrange something. He confided to Richter that Hitler was coming to Karinhalle the following week (probably to put final touches on the invasion of the USSR). Perhaps Richter could conceal himself behind a curtain and at least get a quick sketch of the Führer.

Richter did that, but when Hitler entered the room and the artist looked for the first time directly at that face, his widow later recalled, "My husband said to himself, *'Nein Danke!'*" As an artist he had found nothing worth painting. The face was coarse, banal, "totally uninteresting" — until someone mentioned the word "Jew."

When Hitler heard that word, his face was transformed into something at once demonic and defensive — a transformation that galvanized the artist into action. Richter sketched as rapidly as he could, and then stayed up all night frantically putting it down in oils. The result was a highly unflattering portrayal of the Führer. In order to protect the painting, and himself, Richter did not try to conceal it. He hung it in his studio and labeled it "German Worker on His Wedding Day." Of all his portraits, Richter considered this his masterpiece. The art critic of *Die Zeit* agreed, calling it "the only really authentic portrait of Hitler . . . perhaps the only really authentic portrait that any German artist has ever had the opportunity to paint."

It was exactly what I needed for the cover. This was the portrait I had sought of a psychopathic god. But I had great difficulty getting permission from Herr Niemeyer, the gallery owner. He would not sell it apart from the Göring portrait. The two must go together. I said that I had no interest in buying either one of them, I simply wanted permission to use the Hitler portrait for my book cover. He refused permission. It was only after patient negotiation and considerable expense that Basic Books was able to purchase permission. I had both the title and the picture I wanted.

Visiting Professor
at Texas and Voorhees

Because its historian of Germany was on leave in 1974, the University of Texas at Austin invited me to teach there for a semester. Anne and I drove to Austin from Williamstown. The fuel shortage would mean that New Englanders, who relied heavily on oil for heating their homes, would have trouble keeping warm during the ensuing winter. To save on the consumption of oil and gas, President Nixon declared a highway speed limit of fifty-five miles per hour — a speed Texans found intolerable. The vast expanse of their land seemed to justify the old saying, "The sun is riz, the sun is set — and here we iz in Texas yet."

As soon as we crossed the Texas border we were greeted by bumper stickers: "Drive 85, Help Freeze a Yank." Other signs also caught our attention. On a large barn: "Genuine Antiques Direct, Factory to You." On restaurants: "Guaranteed Cold Ice Water" and "Foot-Long Gourmet Texas Hot Dogs."

We soon discovered that Texans think in superlatives. At a history department reception, I met the father of one of my future colleagues; the older man was from Amarillo, a city in the Texas panhandle. Mr. Jones was greatly impressed with how cold it gets in Amarillo. He explained the phenomenon to me. "That wind just comes a-howlin' down from the Rockies and it is cold, I mean *co-old!* It's the coldest place in the whole state of Texas! I remember as a little nippah being so-o-o cold in Amarillo! Now, where were you bown an' raised?" When I told him I was born and raised in Canada, he didn't like that very much. He said he'd tell me a story:

146

There was these two Texans who were up in that Northwest Territory in one of them iga-loos and they woke up one January mornin' an' theah was a blizzard an', man, it was co-ld an' the wind was a-howlin' 'n' a-blowin' that snow hori-zon-tal.

An' they came out of that iga-loo an' one of 'em stuck his thumb up in the air an' he pulled it right back an' he hunkered down into his fur parka an' he said to his friend, "By da-yumn, Ja-eb, <u>I bet it's cold in Amarillo!</u>"

I had lectured in a German history course on the revolutions of 1848 and talked about the remarkable career of Lola Montez, the "Spanish" dancer who was born in Ireland and became the lover, variously, of two English lords, then Tsar Nicholas I of Russia, Franz Liszt, Honoré de Balzac, Victor Hugo, and the Dumas, *père et fils*. She arrived in Munich and went directly to the office of King Ludwig I, who looked at her famous bosom and asked, "Madam, is that a work of nature or of art?"

Seizing a pair of scissors from his desk, Lola cut open her bodice and replied, "Nature, sire." Ludwig records, "I was bewitched, I know not why." She became the "Uncrowned Queen of Bavaria" and cost Ludwig his throne. Driven out of the country, she, like other gold diggers of 1849, migrated to California. There she established a high-class bordello and endorsed a movement that sought to change the name of the state to Lolaland. Then, at the age of thirty-eight, she experienced a religious conversion and spent the rest of her life beating a drum as she lamented her sins through the streets of New York.

I concluded the lecture by saying that Lola left only two memorials: her name carved on a lonely gravestone in a New York cemetery and emblazoned in neon lights on a tawdry nightclub across from the *Hofbräuhaus* in Munich.

I was mistaken about that. After the lecture on Friday, Anne and I drove through the colorful hill country west of Austin to visit the town of Fredericksburg, which had been settled by German immigrants. I had forgotten to pack a toothbrush — I used one in those days — so we went in search of one in the local Woolworth's. Anne was checking out the junk jewelry and beckoned me to come over. A display of brooches depicting "The Most Beautiful Women of History" included Lola Montez. I bought her brooch for sixty-nine cents and I showed it to my class on Monday, correcting my statement and demonstrating that Lola had not been forgotten in Fredericksburg, Texas.

The Easter vacation at UT did not correspond with the spring break at Voorhees College, a black college in South Carolina. That meant that I could comply with a request that if I could teach at Voorhees for a week, it would greatly help the college remain accredited by having a live Ph.D. on its roster. In my letter of acceptance I said I would not expect any honorarium. If they could provide food and lodging for my wife and me, I would be delighted to come.

We flew to Columbia, rented a car, and drove south on Highway 321 to Voorhees College in the town of Denmark, about ten miles south of Norway, South Carolina. At the administration building we were welcomed by the affable chairman of the history department, who said he would drive us to a Holiday Inn in a neighboring town, where he had reserved accommodations for us. I demurred, saying that would be an unnecessary expense for the college. Could we not be put up in a student dormitory? We were and we got a friendly reception — as well as a prolonged exposure to funk and rock music, at least as loud as it was at Williams and the University of Texas. The difference was that when I commented on the music, the students at Voorhees turned it down after 10 P.M.

Since I had been invited to lecture on "history" for an entire week, I had brought along a large file of notes. After my first talk I shut the file.

My initial appearance was in the college gymnasium before the entire undergraduate body of some 650 African-American students. I have never felt so pale and pink and vulnerable. I said how happy my wife and I were to visit their fine college, that I would just talk for about fifteen minutes and see if I would say something they might like to discuss.

In the course of my remarks, I apparently said that Adolf Hitler has been called a Fascist. When I stopped and asked for their comments, a handsome, very tall, and neatly dressed student rose and said that I had said something that sort of interested him. "You said that Hitler

148

was some sort of fashionist. Now, just what kind of clothes did that dude wear?"

I knew at once that I had misjudged my audience. I apologized for using the wrong word. I should have said "racist" and explained what I meant by that and by "Fascist," certainly not a familiar word.

I could tell that my week at Voorhees would be an educational experience for me. The chairman told me not to assign more than five pages of reading material a day, because most of the students would be reading at about third or fourth grade level. The college had wisely established excellent programs in remedial reading and mathematics. I found most of the students downright eager to learn. Many of the women were going into education, determined, as several told me, to give children a better education than they had received. I am grateful for the experience of teaching such young people.

I had particularly wanted to meet Father Jackson, the Episcopalian chaplain of the college. It was Holy Week, and the bulletin board in front of an attractive stone chapel built by Voorhees students at the turn of the century announced that Father Jackson would lead a worship service on Wednesday at eleven o'clock. Anne and I decided to attend after my ten o'clock class. We constituted the entire congregation.

Shortly after eleven o'clock Father Jackson entered, smiled, and nodded to us. He opened with a prayer and led the congregation in a responsive reading that went rather well. He then announced the first hymn, "Jerusalem the Golden." Anne's contribution was to remain silent. The only tune she could ever carry was "The Isle of Capri," and she knew that her singing would throw off my uncertain "Jerusalem." Fortunately, our duet was led by Father Jackson's confident strong baritone.

When it was time for the sermon, he turned to us and chuckled. "Seeing this congregation, I must say it reminds me of a story." I winced, for I had often heard that line used to introduce a story that had nothing to do with the matter at hand. But his story was perfect for the occasion; it fit like the right key in a lock.

There was, he said, in the deep South and not far from here a young black pastor who had just finished Bible school. He had a parish in a small village and one rural country church. He had carefully prepared his first sermon and was proud of it. He drove his Model T out to the country church and was disappointed to see that the entire congregation consisted of one elderly black farmer. When the time came for the sermon, the young pastor asked for advice from the old man: "Now, Uncle, I have prepared a full sermon, but what do you think I should do?" The old man responded, "Son, when I have a load of hay and I call my mules and only one mule shows up, I feed that mule."

The young pastor felt encouraged. He preached his sermon with confidence and enthusiasm. After the service he met his congregation at the door and asked the old man how he liked the sermon. The old man replied, "I said when I have a load of hay and I call my mules and only one mule turns up, I feed that mule. I don't dump the whole load on him!"

Father Jackson said, "Now, folks, I won't dump the whole load on you, but this is about what I was going to say." He then gave a clear five-minute précis of an excellent homily. He invited us to his home for tea and we spent a delightful half hour with him and his charming wife.

Anne and I were moved by the number of students who showed up for the farewell tea given for us. I consider my week of teaching at Voorhees College among the most rewarding weeks of my academic career.

SOVIET RUSSIA BY BUS:
"Who Knows?"

Back in Austin, we saw in a travel agency an advertisement for a bus trip through the Soviet Union. The bus would leave from Victoria Station, London, cross the Channel to Ostend, pick up a Dutch bus and driver for the trip, cross East Germany to Berlin, proceed to Warsaw, Minsk, and Smolensk and up to Moscow. We would then take a train to Leningrad, board a Soviet ship to sail the Baltic and North Seas and back to London.

We joined a friendly group of twenty excited people. Anne and I and a conservative Republican couple from California were the only Americans. There were four Canadians, eight Australians, and one Indian from Calcutta; the rest were West Germans. There was no toilet on the bus, and the one public lavatory we visited along the road in the USSR was so filthy that we preferred birch groves: men to the right, women to the left.

One of the Canadians enjoyed kidding an enormous Australian cattleman about his very broad accent. What, he asked, is the difference between a bison and a buffalo? The Aussie thought for a minute and replied, "No diff'rence, mite, no diff'rence at all." The Canadian insisted there was a great difference: A buffalo was a large land mammal that roamed the plains of North America. The Aussie said, "Right. And what's a bison, then? Sime thing!" The Canadian replied, "Oh, no it isn't! A bison is what you Aussies wash your fice in." We narrowly avoided a homicide on the bus.

In Minsk we displayed a graphic example of human cupidity. We were put up at a clean and comfortable Intourist hotel. On a side table in our room was a dish with two beautiful apples. At supper we said

151

how pleased we had been to find the apples. Another couple at our table also remarked that they, too, had been given apples and thought it a nice touch. We were completely happy until a third couple said that they had been given apples and also a pear. Our immediate reaction: How come we got only apples?

In Warsaw we paid our respects at the impressive monument to the heroic dead of the Warsaw Ghetto and marveled at the incredibly detailed and accurate restoration of the old city after the Nazi devastation. We were served in a tea shop by a voluble Pole who had flown with the RAF during the war and who despised the Russians who were now occupying his country. Two stolid, bullet-headed officers of the Red Army were drinking tea at a corner table. Our waiter told us that he had just had some fun with them. They had never seen teabags before, and were highly suspicious of them. "What," they asked, "do you do with those little bags?" "That's the way we make tea." "How do you make tea that way?" "We put the bag in our mouth and pour in very hot water."

The waiter said he gave them water as hot as he dared and watched with great pleasure as the Soviets, determined to prove they were tougher than the Poles, sat stolidly with their beet-red faces puffed out as steam escaped from their ears.

Our bus trip had been organized and promoted jointly by Thomas Cook and Intourist, the official Soviet tourist agency. Our Intourist guide was a young, physically attractive but humorless Communist fanatic named Olga. She wore boots and a leather miniskirt to show off her legs. Thomas Cook was represented by a harried and hirsute Oxonian named Keith, who had read history at Keble College. When we arrived in Moscow, he suggested that he and I go to the Kazan Railway Station, where we would see something interesting.

On any given day, there are about nine million people in the city of Moscow. Approximately one million of them are visitors. Ordinary sightseers, devout Orthodox Christians come to genuflect in the sacred Kremlin and to hear Mass in its great churches, and equally devout Communists come to genuflect as they gaze on the remains of St. Vladimir Lenin.

In the enormous Kazan station — three or four times the size of Grand Central — hundreds and hundreds of these Russians were waiting for the train that would take them home to villages and towns strung across the vast space of the steppes. Many had been waiting for days — waiting because the exact time their train would leave was not posted. Railway time schedules were a state secret in the Soviet Union. So people waited until the train they wanted was suddenly announced. Elderly grandparents, cripples, young parents with little children were all sitting or lying on the floor of the vast station. No seats or benches were provided. It was this scene of massed and disciplined humanity that Keith thought I would find interesting. I found it one more example — like the lack of public conveniences along the great highways — of the state's indifference to the comfort of individual citizens in what they were pleased to call the People's Republic.

We found the Kirov performance of *Swan Lake* so enchanting that it made comparison with any future performance invidious. The Moscow Circus had a similar effect on future circuses. We had had a remarkably rich trip but were glad it was drawing to a close.

We had traveled light. Anne and I shared one soft under-the-seat flight bag, and we each carried a small backpack. I took two books — the New Testament and Joachim Fest's fine 1,000-page *Hitler: Eine Biographie* — my needlepoint, a recorder and a thin pamphlet of sheet music, and a map. Therein lies a tale.

Before leaving Williamstown, I had consulted a colleague who was a specialist in Soviet history about a street map of Moscow. I wanted to locate several palaces, monasteries, and churches that I intended to visit. He told me I couldn't rely on the Intourist maps — they were all deliberately inaccurate. He recommended that I enlarge and photocopy the 1914 Baedeker map of Moscow. He went over the map with me and together we marked with red Xs the places I intended to visit. To keep the map flat, I placed it in my book of recorder sheet music.

Our long bus ride had ended in Moscow. We were to take the train to Leningrad and then embark on a Soviet ship. We were given strict instructions to leave our suitcases on our bed in the Leningrad hotel room. Soviet porters would see that they were delivered to the pier, where we would retrieve them for our Baltic cruise and return to London.

As soon as we arrived at the point of debarkation, Olga directed us to the shed where the luggage was lined up on a long table. Our bag was not there. I reported that fact to Olga. She was furious. A Muscovite who had a boyfriend in Moscow, she wanted nothing better than to get back home. Her responsibilities would be over as soon as she got rid of us by putting us on a Soviet boat. She told me, "What you say is not possible. Your bag is where it should be." I replied, "You have been telling us for a week that everything is possible in the USSR; this is one of the possible things. Our bag is not there. Please come and look for yourself." She looked. It was not there.

She escorted me to the office of the Port Commissar, a quintessential Soviet bureaucrat. Olga reported the lost bag. He telephoned someone and talked rapidly in Russian. He rang another number, talked rapidly again, and hung up. He told Anne and me to return in ten minutes. The ship was now tooting its all-aboard whistle.

In ten minutes we returned to the Commissar and the following conversation took place.

> *He:* We have found your bag.
> *I:* I am pleased to hear that.
> *He:* (darkly) Do you know what we think?
> *I:* I have no idea what you think.
> *He:* We think you hid your bag.
> *I:* We did what? That is the only bag we have! Why would we want to hide it?
> *He:* (suspiciously) Who knows?

In our cabin we searched the bag carefully. The Baedeker map with its red markings had been removed.

OXFORD:

"I'm Afraid I Shall Have to Battel You" and Two Historians

After my stint at UT Austin and the publication of my Hitler book in 1977, I was invited to St. Antony's College, Oxford, as a Senior Associate Member (a SAM, in local parlance). St. Antony's is one of the newer and livelier of the Oxford colleges. It was established in the 1930s by a wealthy French Oxonian who believed that history should continue past Edwardian England and the outbreak of the Great War. He thought it time that attention was paid to the rest of the twentieth century. The college is divided into various centers that concentrate on such areas as European studies, African studies, Asian studies, Russian and East European studies, and so on. Students are graduates. I participated in the German seminar under the superb leadership of A. C. Nicholls.

I was particularly pleased to be at St. Antony's because I was beginning my study of Kaiser Wilhelm II, and the late Sir John Wheeler-Bennett, a former Fellow of the college who had planned a biography of the Kaiser, had left a considerable amount of material to his college when he retired. It included his account of visiting the ex-Kaiser during his exile in Doorn in August 1939, just before the outbreak of the Second World War.

First I had to learn some new English words. I had gone to the bursar's office and asked a tiny, prim, elderly lady if I might have a few sheets of college stationery. She said, "Yes, I think that can be arranged; you are our new SAM, aren't you? Would five sheets do?" She surprised me by commenting, "I'm afraid I shall have to *battel* you for them." I knew I was a bit past my prime, but since she didn't look at all pugnacious and couldn't have weighed more than ninety-seven pounds, I agreed. But I must have looked puzzled, for she explained that she was going to put the charges on my "battels," Oxonian for my account.

We rented a small cottage — a "terrace house" — on Plantation Road, a five-minute walk from the college. To have Anne's relatives visit us there was pleasant, though crowded. They did not stay long, perhaps because I had become fond of haggis, which I could get from a Scots butcher in the Covered Market. The second night I served haggis and neeps (turnips) to my in-laws; the third night they took us out to dinner; they left the next morning.

During my first year at Oxford in 1978, I met two famous historians of very different qualities and temperament: Alan Bullock and Hugh Trevor-Roper.

Shortly after I arrived, I received a luncheon invitation from Lord Bullock and was asked to meet him in the Master's lodgings at St. Catherine's College. Bullock had been Vice-Chancellor of Oxford University (1954–73) before becoming Master of St. Catherine's. Among other books, he had written a fine political biography of Adolf Hitler that had gone through many editions. He had been very kind to me, having given my Hitler book a remarkably warm and generous review in the *New York Review of Books.*

Since he had a later appointment that day, could I come as early as 11:30 so that we could have a sherry in his rooms before going into lunch?

I found him to be of short and stocky stature, engaging humor, bristling mustache, and twinkling eye. We had a relaxed and congenial half hour cordially disagreeing about our differing interpretations of Hitler. Then he walked me over to the dining hall and introduced me to a Fellow who would be my host at High Table, since Bullock had to leave. Several days later I learned from a secretary that Bullock's later appointment that day had been to make a rather important speech in the House of Lords. It occurred to me that a lesser person would have mentioned that fact in the course of our conversation.

Hugh Trevor-Roper was very different. I had corresponded with him and appeared with him during a panel discussion. Two days later, while I was showing the Bodleian Library to an American historian who had read some of Trevor-Roper's brilliant books, the great man himself entered, dressed dramatically in an Inverness cape and deerstalker hat. When my friend expressed a desire to meet him, I took my visitor by the elbow and ushered him toward Trevor-Roper. When he saw us approaching, he looked right through me and kept on walking. I felt cut off at the ankles. When I told a friend at St. Antony's what had happened, he said he was not at all surprised. "Trevor-Roper does that all the time," he said. "He is intolerable."

In 1947, though he was noted as a scholar of eighteenth-century England, Trevor-Roper had been assigned by the British Army to find out what had actually happened to Hitler. He had interviewed all available live witnesses and gained international fame by writing a superb reconstruction entitled *The Last Days of Hitler,* which subsequently went through many editions.

Then, many years later, he achieved notoriety by trying to authenticate the so-called "Hitler Diaries." Anybody who really knew Hitler well as a person would know that he could not possibly have written that extensive diary, but Trevor-Roper — now Lord Dacre and Master of Peterhouse, Cambridge — announced flatly, "The diaries are genuine. I stake my reputation on it."

When, a few days later, the diaries were proven to be a complete fraud, many of his colleagues were delighted to see the egg on Lord Dacre's face, and one of his new Cantabridgean colleagues must have enjoyed penning the following lines:

An exalted Master named Dacre
Was god in his own little acre,
But in matters of diaries
He was quite ultra vires,
Quite unable to spot an old faker.

The Oxford connection helped me gain access to important documents regarding Wilhelm II's childhood. His mother, Victoria, had been the Princess Royal, the eldest daughter of Queen Victoria and Prince Albert. At the age of eighteen she had married the Prussian prince who would become the future Kaiser Friedrich III, Emperor of Germany. Princess Victoria, or Vicky, as she was called in the family, did not keep a diary, but virtually every day from 1858 to 1901 she wrote long, self-revealing letters to "Dear Mama," Queen Victoria. Thousands of these letters are written in Vicky's clear, legible hand — in contrast to the queen's undecipherable scrawl — on good paper, bound in leather volumes and kept in the private Royal Archives in the round tower of Windsor Castle. One must get permission from Queen Elizabeth II to read her great-great-aunt's correspondence. I used one of my few sheets of St. Antony's College stationery to obtain that permission.

Every day for a week, a war-decorated warden opened the massive outer door with his enormous key and let me into the Round Tower so I could climb the 150 — as I recall — deeply worn circular stone steps leading to the archives. Charming elderly women brought me volumes of letters to read and served me tea and biscuits at midmorning and late afternoon.

The letters are fascinating. They reveal a gifted, strong-willed, and terribly lonely teenager who is appalled that the child she has borne, after a harrowing breech delivery, has been left with a badly deformed left arm — an incurable condition that Vicky refuses to accept. She tells her mother all about the well-meaning tortures she inflicts daily on little Willie in desperate and futile efforts to make him as physically "perfect" as her own adored father, Prince Albert. She has strapped the good arm down, for instance, to force the infant to use the useless one; she has designed a harness and crank to straighten out a deformed shoulder; she has dozens of live rabbits split open and forces the infant to hold his arm in their entrails in the hope that daily exposure to animal heat will cure the arm; she has the arm wired so that she can supervise daily electric shock treatment, battling daily with pediatricians who warn her that no one knows what physical and mental damage might result from these mysterious new "galvanic impulses." Over the objections of her doctors and the screams of her child, she continues the "treatments" because it "is for Willie's own good." There is no doubt that she loved her baby and meant well, but many years later the ex-Kaiser, exiled in Doorn, told Wheeler-Bennett, "My childhood was one long torture."

Every evening after the Royal Archives closed, I took the shuttle train from the Windsor-Eton station to Slough, where I could catch the through train to London. Across the aisle from me, one evening, an American couple with New York accents looked out the window as the train curved past Windsor Castle. We saw the declining rays of the sun catch the pennants gently waving over the massive Round Tower, constructed originally by William the Conqueror shortly after his conquest of England. I overheard their conversation:

He: Now there, Mabel, is a castle!

She: Yeah, Irving, it is a castle.

He: (after a long, reflective pause) You know what, Mabel? I do not wish to hoit their feelinks. I do not wish to hoit their feelinks. But for my part, for castles, I'll take Disneyland.

EMERGENCY ROOM, RADCLIFFE INFIRMARY

One misty April morning in 1982, I was cycling as usual from our flat on Leckford Road to the Bodleian Library. As I wheeled thoughtfully down St. Giles and approached Broad Street, I suddenly lost control of the bike. It wobbled all over the street as the world whirled about me. I managed to walk the bike to the cycle park near the Bodleian, but as I started up the steps to the Lower Reading Room, my legs acted as if their owner were thoroughly intoxicated. I sat down on the library steps and then somehow — I don't remember much of this — walked the bicycle home and blacked out in our flat. Anne called the college physician, who stethoscoped me and made two telephone calls. I found myself first in an ambulance and then the cardiac emergency room of the University teaching hospital, the Radcliffe Infirmary.

There I had joined a dozen other patients who were wired to individual machines that blipped and flashed all night. My spirits were not raised when I noticed that two of my roommates had expired during the early morning hours and had been quietly wheeled down to the morgue.

I prayed to the God who had sustained me so often in the past and a great peace came over me. I knew all would be well.

I spent a week being monitored and investigated by medical students. After three days I felt vigorous enough to complain about the food and to rejoice when the kitchen staff went on strike and the infirmary was forced to work a deal with British Air to supply us with airplane food — a very considerable improvement over our usual fare of boiled tripe, overcooked Brussels sprouts, tired "toad-in-the-hole" (bits of pork sausage floating greasily in a thick pancake), and overdone "bubble-and-squeak" (vegetables thoroughly fried in lard).

Anne visited every day, bringing me joy and food supplements. At the end of the week the Sister in charge of the ward informed me that I could go home. Recalling the lengthy financial negotiations before one could leave an American hospital, I asked her about the procedure for dismissal. She smiled and said, "Well, if I were you, I should proceed to the clothes press, put on my trousers and walk out of here." It was as simple and cost-free as that. That evening Anne and I raised a grateful toast to National Health.

In Pursuit of the Kaiser at Doorn

In a driving rain on the night of 10–11 November 1918, when Kaiser Wilhelm II fled from Germany, he was offered sanctuary in Holland by Queen Wilhelmina. She had prevailed upon Godard Bentinck Graaf van Oldenburg-Bentinck, the head of a distinguished Dutch-German-English family, to invite the Kaiser to stay in his château in Amerongen.

The count reluctantly agreed, provided the Dutch government pay for the food and fuel consumed by the Kaiser and his entourage. (Wilhelm had arrived with a retinue of 79 servants; they would soon be followed by a tea set for 200 people.) The count and countess had understood that their guests would stay for three days; they were to stay for eighteen months.

Finally, in May 1920, the Kaiser purchased a newly renovated former castle that had previously been owned by Audrey Hepburn's grandmother. It was complete with moat, drawbridge, and some 169 acres of woodland and pasture. The ex-Kaiser renamed his handsome estate Huis Doorn (Doorn House). Three years after Wilhelm died in 1941, his eldest son, who along with a younger brother had joined Hitler's Brown Shirts, wanted to sell the property to raise money for Hitler's war effort during the late stages of the Second World War. The Dutch government scotched that deal by buying the entire property from the ex-Kaiser's estate and converting it into a well-maintained national museum.

In the spring of 1990 I had written to L. J. Verroen, the Archivist and Curator of Doorn House, asking if I could visit the Kaiser's library and archives. A gracious and helpful letter in response told me that the house would be closed for a year, beginning in mid-June, while it was undergoing a complete renovation. If I wished to visit, I should come very soon. Anne and I left the following week.

We booked a room in a tidy pension just across the road from the Doorn House gate. I called on Mr. Verroen that afternoon. He welcomed me, showed me around the ground floor of the house, which is normally opened to visitors, and then apologized, saying he had to be away to meetings the next day, and wondered if I would mind looking after myself. The Kaiser's private apartment, study, and bedroom, not normally open to visitors, would be made available to me. Most of the Kaiser's books and paintings were now stored in the Gate House; I could get to them later.

I was delighted. I don't remember spending a more exciting and pleasant day walking slowly and alone through visible history.

In a closet I found some of the Kaiser's watercolors, which were quite good — about the caliber of Hitler's paintings. I also found a striking black-and-white sketch of the Kaiser's beloved grandfather, old Kaiser Wilhelm I, as he lay on his deathbed. The drawing is impressive. It reminded me that Adolf Hitler had also stayed in his mother's bedroom the night she died, and he drew her frail body as it was wasted by cancer.

In an attic closet I found a box of miscellaneous items that included a swastika medallion that, for a time, had been attached to the radiator of the Kaiser's Mercedes. He had had it removed when all hope that Hitler might restore the monarchy was lost.

In another closet I discovered hundreds of copies of a pamphlet entitled *Die Weltkrieglüge (The World War Lie),* designed to prove that Germany was not responsible for the Great War. I also found a box containing unused copies of the postcard the German government had sent by the hundreds to the United States in 1915 in an effort to encourage American neutrality during the war. Next to the colored portrait of the Kaiser in full uniform are the words *"Vor Gott und der Geschichte ist mein Gewissen rein. Ich habe den Krieg nicht gewolt. Wilhelm II I.R."* (Before God and History, my conscience is clear. I did not want this war. Wilhelm II I.R.).

There is particular poignancy in the copy of this card that I hold in my hand as I write these lines. It was given to me by a Jewish friend who had found it among her mother's effects. The message was written by a young Jewish soldier in November 1915. In addition to sending his mother "warmest birthday greetings," he expressed his confidence in the "quick and glorious victory of German arms." The card was sent from Theresienstadt. During the Third Reich that place would become a concentration camp for Jews en route to Auschwitz.

The Kaiser's large bedroom has been left the way it was the night he died on 4 June 1941. Over his bed is a portrait of his first wife at the time of their marriage; on one wall hangs an excellent copy of Cranach's *Martin Luther;* and on his bedside table are pamphlets of Lutheran prayers and devotional readings.

His study is magnificently situated atop the castle's tower, with large windows facing in all directions. At his desk an English riding saddle, in place of a chair, is mounted on a piano-stool type of spool that enables the saddle to be raised and lowered — presumably so the Kaiser could raise his royal presence above his visitors. (All his offices were fitted with similar saddles.) I found the one at Doorn quite comfortable.

I spent several days going through the sermons the Kaiser preached and the scholarly archaeological papers he wrote. The first drafts of his writing show revisions that made his prose more vigorous and effective — a concern about language and style that was lacking in Hitler's writing.

I browsed for several hours through the Kaiser's private library of some 5,000 volumes now housed over the Gate House. I was amused to find that a letter written by the young Prince Wilhelm that I had read in the Royal Archives was graphically contradicted by the evidence before my eyes. In the letter Willie had written to Queen Victoria, he thanked her profusely for sending him a presentation copy of Prince Albert's huge official biography. He assured his grandmother that "it is my favourite reading." Each of the five volumes in Doorn House is inscribed "To darling Willie with love from Grandmama" — and in each the pages remain uncut!

Other books caught my eye. I noticed that in contrast to Hitler's personal library, which I had also examined, there are copies of the classics of world literature in four languages, as well as books on subjects ranging from philosophy and religion to art, physics, city planning, and archaeology. Like Hitler, he was fascinated by racism and the occult. He was also a fan of Dorothy Sayers.

The Kaiser kept meticulous records of all his guests at Doorn House. We know their names and titles, what they ate, what kinds and how much wine they drank, how long the guests stayed, and the topics of their conversations. He also recorded the number of parties he gave for the children of the village of Doorn — one can understand why he was such a well-liked old gentleman in the village and was greeted respectfully as he went on his walks, swinging the walking stick once owned by Frederick the Great. The Kaiser also kept track of all the birthdays and the gifts he had given both to his extended family and to his servants and retainers. One notebook lists the trees he cut down in his forest. By 5 December 1920, for example, he had already cut down and sawed up more than 13,000 trees (presumably, many of them were saplings).

I found enormous scrapbooks that contained yellowing newspaper clippings from the world's newspapers: from London, New York, Paris, Berlin, Moscow, but also from New Delhi, Sophia, Istanbul, Cape Town, Boston, Dublin, Prague. He followed with particular care such events as Lindbergh's flight and the kidnapping of the Lindbergh baby, Gandhi's campaign against the British Raj, and Adolf Hitler's trial for treason in February 1924 for the Beer Hall Putsch of 1923. Wilhelm applauded Hitler's defense, noting in a margin of one paper, "He is a fine German patriot who only wants to restore German honor."

During the Second World War, the German High Command sent the ex-Kaiser daily bulletins on the *Wehrmacht*'s progress. He received the last bulletin on the day he died, 4 June 1941.

DR. JOHNSON AND MY TAPESTRY

Anne and I were fortunate that for both years I was at Oxford, friends in the U.S. Embassy gave us the key to the "servants' quarters," complete with kitchen, in their Embassy House off Sloane Square. That meant we could spend long weekends, at very little expense, in London.

One gloomy September afternoon, we had visited Dr. Johnson's home and had seen the huge padlock and chain he had ordered so that he could be manacled in the event that he went insane, as he desperately feared he might. We also examined a copy of his famous dictionary. This first proper dictionary of the English language, this creation of one man, has been called the single greatest intellectual achievement of one person in Western history.

That Dr. Johnson was a stickler for the accurate use of words was illustrated one hot and humid evening in St. Clement Danes, the Anglican parish church he regularly attended. There, during one especially uncomfortable Evensong, the woman sitting next to the habitually unwashed Johnson could not stand it any longer. She turned to him and said, "Excuse me, Dr. Johnson, but you *smell.*" "No, madam," the venerable doctor replied equably, "You smell that I *stink.*"

Anne and I continued our walk rather aimlessly in east London, when I saw a building with the words carved in stone above its portal "Municipal Court of Criminal Justice." I said, "Hey, that's Old Bailey! Let's go in and listen to a trial." The decorated beadle ushered us to a seat in the front row of the steeply tiered spectators' gallery. Directly across and down from us sat the jury, to our right the prisoner in the dock, to our left His Lordship in wig and scarlet gown. Since I secretly harbored Walter Mitty dreams of being an attorney, I was fascinated by the eloquence of the barristers. The multicultured jury was especially interesting to me. I looked down at them with interest, and they looked up at me with considerable curiosity, for they saw a bearded man doing needlepoint, a habit I had originally acquired in 1974 for taking that bus trip through the Soviet Union and continued as a way to survive faculty meetings at Williams College.

The trial was becoming more and more exciting, and I was plying my needle to keep pace with the mounting tension. Suddenly, an interval of silence was broken by His Lordship's stentorian voice: *"The bearded gentleman in the front row of the gallery will put away his tapestry immediately. He is distracting the attention of our jurors!"*

The bearded gentleman, who had no difficulty identifying the culprit, complied at once; his wife looked as if she had never in her life seen him.

After another rewarding weekend in London, one Sunday afternoon we took the Oxford Express bus from Victoria Coach Station. The coach was so full we were lucky to get separate seats. I sat next to an attractive dark young woman who told me she was from Egypt and was visiting Oxford for the first time. She had come to stay with her husband, who was attending Trinity College. As we entered the city on the London Road, I was telling her something about the college system and the dates of their founding. As a son of the North American Midwest, I was impressed with their antiquity, and waxed enthusiastic in what turned into a lecture: "That's the famous spire of Magdalen, sometimes called the most beautiful spire in England, established 1458. . . Beyond to the east is New College; actually, it was founded in 1379!" And as we drove up the High, "Off to the west is Merton College, established 1264; it was really the first college in the modern sense; its organizational form became the model for others. And there's 'Univ.' — really University College — founded 1249. Isn't that amazing? *1249!*"

The young Egyptian smiled quietly and asked, "Before Christ?"

Tel Aviv, L.A. Rams, and Jerusalem

In 1982 the International Scholars' Conference on the Holocaust and Genocide was held in Tel Aviv. I received a letter at Oxford inviting me to give a paper on "Hitler and the Holocaust." Fortunately, I had that letter in my pocket as Anne and I checked in at the El Al counter in Heathrow. During the very careful scrutiny of our person and our baggage, I was asked why I was traveling to Israel. I replied that I was going to give a paper at a conference on the Holocaust in Tel Aviv. The woman at the counter said, "There is no such conference in Tel Aviv."

I expressed surprise and showed her my letter. It was her turn to be surprised; she took the letter to her supervisor, and after an extensive conference, we were allowed to board the plane. The mystery remained. On arrival in Tel Aviv we found that our reservations at a conference hotel were in order. The next day I went to conference headquarters and discovered that many of the scheduled papers had inexplicably been canceled. Cancellations included the opening address by Elie Wiesel and a paper by Robert Lifton, M.D., of Yale, who had been scheduled to talk on SS doctors and the Holocaust. My paper, along with several others, was scheduled, with the time and the room given.

I encountered a gentile friend who had helped organize the conference and asked what was going on. Was there, in fact, a conference? Was he going to give his paper? Should I give mine? He said that he had heard that the Turkish government objected to a paper that was slated to be given by a distinguished Armenian scholar entitled "The Armenian Massacre of 1915," because Turkey still refuses to admit that such a massacre ever took place.

Despite this denial, the facts about the massacres are incontrovertible. Between 1915 and 1917 the Turkish government planned and perpetrated the first government-directed genocide of the twentieth century.

Early in 1915 the government established a "Special Organization" *(Testshkilat-i Mahsusa)* charged with organizing and supervising the systematic massacres. They took place in three stages. First, in April 1915, religious, educational, professional, and intellectual leaders throughout the Turkish Empire were arrested and executed — a precursor of Nazi efforts to wipe out Polish leaders. Second, Armenian draftees in the Turkish army, about 200,000 men, were executed. Third, the remainder of the Armenian population, largely elderly people, women, and children, were forced to go on death marches into the desert, where, by the hundreds of thousands, they died of exhaustion, dehydration, hunger, disease, and outright murder.

The impact on the Armenian people was devastating. Of the two to three million Western Armenians living in the Turkish Empire in 1915, at least one and a half million perished by 1917 during this Turkish holocaust.

When the Turkish government, still flatly denying those facts, discovered that a paper was to be given on the subject during a conference in Tel Aviv in 1982, it informed the Israeli government that if it did not cancel the entire conference, the Turkish government would "not be responsible for the safety" of Jews who had fled to Turkey to escape persecution in Iran.

The Jewish organizers of the conference met in emergency session. They could not reach agreement. Many members, fearing for the lives of fellow Jews in Turkey, wanted to cancel the conference. Others, refusing to submit to what they considered a form of blackmail, insisted that the conference must proceed as scheduled. It was decided that the Israeli government should officially declare the conference closed, but papers could be given unofficially. I, along with most of the other gentiles at the conference — not knowing then about the Turkish threat — went ahead and delivered our papers. The attendance at all those sessions, considering the circumstances, was surprisingly good.

I learned later that Jewish participants had all received letters informing them of the Turkish threat and were asked individually if they wished to participate. Elie Wiesel told me some months later that he and other Jews had declined to participate because they had not wanted to feel responsible for the possible deaths of fellow Jews. I could understand his thinking, but I expressed regret that the leaders of the conference had not informed me and other gentiles of the problem so that we, too, could have made our own decisions. He agreed with me and said that I should have been informed.

For this international conference, publishing houses from many countries displayed their books and monographs on the Holocaust. With a colleague from Hebrew University I walked slowly past a table piled high with hundreds of titles. He commented ironically, "Yeah, there's no business like Shoah business." Since 1982 the number of volumes on the Holocaust has at least quadrupled.

While in Tel Aviv, Anne and I strolled along the Mediterranean shore and watched a group of teenagers horsing around. One of the boys was wearing a Los Angeles Rams T-shirt. I asked him how things were in L.A. He didn't know what I was talking about. He and his friends, who were anxious to try out their English, bombarded us with questions about teenage life in the States. One question was particularly interesting: Were there any Jews in America? I said indeed there were. Did I know any personally? I said that indeed I did. Did they talk Hebrew? I replied that they were bar or bas mitzvahed, but I'm sure they didn't talk Hebrew every day. "Well," was the response, "then they are not Jews." It was a definition I had not heard before.

We had not found the city of Tel Aviv particularly interesting and looked forward to spending a week in Jerusalem, where we had booked a room in the YMCA in the Arab quarter a few short blocks from the Damascus Gate into the old city. We found the sights and smells and memories of the old city fascinating and spent hours every day walking through it. On the Via Dolorosa my pocket was picked, I suspect by an Italian pilgrim.

The Patriarch of the Christian Armenian Church had invited to a reception all those who had participated in the Tel Aviv conference. It was a lavish affair. From his throne on a dais the Patriarch greeted us individually and bestowed a blessing. The buffet that followed was elaborate, the roast lamb especially memorable, the wines and rare liqueurs superb.

Because of the Israeli "incursion" into Lebanon, airport security was especially tight. We were told to report to Ben Gurion Airport at least two hours before our flight to London, the only flight leaving Israel. That meant we had to get up at 3:30 A.M. to get the cab that would pick us up at four o'clock. The Arab at the desk promised by Allah and all that was holy he would personally wake us promptly at 3:30. He never showed up. Fortunately, I happened to wake at 3:45. I aroused Anne and, in a sleepy panic, she stumbled around the room, mumbling, "I knew that Jasper wouldn't wake us up. Now what are we going to do?"

The *sherut* was very late, but driving at speeds in excess of 150 kilometers an hour in the big Mercedes, the driver delivered his nerve-damaged passengers to Ben Gurion in time to catch the only plane to London, thence back to Oxford.

FILMMAKING IN ALASKA

After the war, one of my colleagues teaching History 1 at Harvard was a delightful Scot with a lovely burred accent and an engaging sense of humor named David Elliot. The scene now shifts to Williams College many years later. One afternoon in September 1971, a knock at my office door admitted a merry-eyed, young woman who said, "I'm Nan Elliot, David Elliot's daughter, and he tells me I should take some history courses with you." She decided to study Russian and German history with me.

Such was my introduction to one of the most exciting, gifted, gutsy, and creative persons I have ever known. After she graduated from Williams in 1973, we kept in touch with annual Christmas letters. She went to Alaska and, like many young people, fell in love with the place.

She climbed its mountains; she flew with bush pilots to villages on its far northern shores; she ran the Iditarod; she slept with Inuit families in igloos in Alaska and with coal miners' families in Appalachia; she lived and climbed with Sherpas in the Himalayas, she filmed Japanese fishing crews in the Pacific. She served as foreign correspondent in Sri Lanka, Nepal, India, and Japan; she wrote four fine books; she produced award-winning films for public television; she kayaked more than 500 miles through the Gulf of Alaska.

One day in 1984 Nan telephoned me from Anchorage and said I was the only person who could rescue her from dire distress. I told her I could not imagine any distress with which she could not cope. She said she had been commissioned to produce a five-part show for public television on the history of Alaska, that part two concerned the Russian occupation and that she wanted me to check the script and do the narration for the film. She would make me the Alistair Cooke of Alaska. I thanked her kindly but said there were three compelling reasons why she should get someone else. *One:* There are hundreds of historians in the Western world who know more about Russian Alaska than I, and that at least a dozen lived in Alaska. *Two:* I was up to my neck in my book comparing Kaiser and Führer, and both of them were commanding all my nonteaching time. *Three:* I did not want to be the Alistair Cooke of Alaska, I just wanted to be the Robert Waite of Williamstown.

She told me that this was the opportunity of a lifetime to see the most marvelous place on earth; that Anne could go too; that I would be on location wherever the Russians had done interesting things; that I would have ample time off while she was setting up locations; that she would lend me her car; that she would not be able to pay an honorarium but she would pay our travel and lodging expenses. She told me to think of Anne in all this and that we would all have great fun together. I agreed to go.

We were fascinated by Alaska. I found Sitka, once the Russian capital city, particularly appealing. Not, however, for the climate. We arrived on Bastille Day and noted a sign in the bookstore: "Please don't drip on our books." Shops sold T-shirts with the message "Sitka Rain Festival: January 1–December 31."

Early in the eighteenth century, the Russian Orthodox Bishop Innocent (Ivan Veniaminov), later canonized as St. Innocent, translated the New Testament into Aleut, built chapels and schools and the handsome wooden St. Michael's Cathedral. When Anne and I attended services there one Sunday, we were the only Caucasians present. The priest, a native Indian in full Orthodox regalia, chanted in Russian and swung a censer that thoroughly incensed us. The service was conducted in Russian, of which I could catch a word or two, but the sermon was completely unintelligible. It was preached in Aleut. After the service we remained to talk with the priest and to admire the priceless icons, encased in pure silver and brought from Russia in the eighteenth century.

One of the key locations in the film was the remains of a stone fortress the Russians had built atop Castle Hill in Sitka to defend their capital from Tlingit Indian attack. Here I was supposed to deliver a major spiel about the savage conflict between Russians and native Indians, and here I was destined to swear that never again would I step in front of a movie camera.

Because we needed to start filming before 4:30 A.M. to avoid competition from city garbage collectors, our day began at 3:30. On location one goof followed another; we required eight or nine takes. I forgot to plug in my microphone; the camera ran out of film; workmen started to sandblast a nearby bridge; a garbage truck clanked by.

One of my best lines went like this: "This fortress was built to defend the capital the Russians called *Novyi Arkangelsk* (New Archangel). But the natives preferred to call it by a quaint old Tlingit name, Simca, meaning 'place by the sea.'"

Simca, of course, means nothing of the kind. It comes from a quaint old French word meaning automobile. At least three times, when everything else was all set, I persisted in saying, "they preferred to call it Simca," requiring a new take each time. Nan finally rescued the enterprise by standing behind the camerman with a quickly improvised cardboard sign reading in all caps a foot high: SIDKA, at long last I managed to master the word.

I had virtually nothing to do with the film's winning seven national and international prizes, including the Golden Eagle Award for the best educational film produced for public television in 1986. The award was won by Nan Elliot for the ingenious way she combined memoirs, letters and diaries of settlers and Russian governors, old newsreels, early daguerreotypes, photographs, and brilliant photography, all joined together by a script of lucid and engaging prose.

March in Portal, Arizona

T. S. Eliot got his months mixed up. At least in Williamstown, March and not April is the cruelest month. To escape its relentlessly dark and dripping days, every March Anne and I drove to Cave Creek Canyon in the Chiricahua Mountains of southeastern Arizona, where the air was dry, the sky blue, and spring flowers were blooming along the roaring brook that for centuries had carved its way through the mountains to leave a verdant band in the desert. The creek had also carved caves in the limestone mountains where prehistoric Indians had left cryptic messages and mysterious paintings.

Our cabin, 5,000 feet above sea level, was located about two miles from the hamlet of Portal, Arizona. Let me locate Portal for you. It is about five miles east of Paradise, Arizona, and sixty miles north of Douglas on the Mexican border — the location of the nearest proper grocery store — and six miles west of Rodeo, New Mexico.

You know when you are in Paradise because there are six mailboxes, two long-abandoned sod shanties, and one peacock farm with some fifty peacocks. I never discovered why anyone would want to raise these foul-smelling, raucous-voiced, dimwitted, constantly shitting birds who seldom fan out their gorgeous tails.

Rodeo was once a thriving cattle-shipping town, a busy railway center with three churches and five whorehouses. It now has one church, a small art gallery, and a general store with one gas pump that sells bumper stickers with the legend, "Happiness Is Seeing Rodeo NM in Your Rear-View Mirror."

Portal had a population of about 150 people, a former one-room school (now a lending library staffed by volunteers), a U.S. post office and general store, a small café, and a tavern with a pool table. Attached to the pull cord that activated the pool-table light was the whitened skull of a javelina — a vicious wild pig with murderous tusks. On the skull was printed in black letters "I cheated at pool."

I spent mornings writing while Anne painted or went on bird walks with friends. The canyon is a world-famous sanctuary with some twenty kinds of hummingbirds and many varieties of parrots, including the rare Coppery-Tailed Elegant Trogon. Once a week or so we would walk to Portal to get a fresh supply of library books and have a beer and a Tex-Mex supper at the Portal Cafe. We would return to read by a mesquite fire or take our sleeping bags out under the desert sky with millions of stars shining in the thin, clear mountain air, so bright and so close to us we felt we could reach up and grab a handful.

LAKE TEMAGAMI AND POLAR BEARS

For a week or two almost every August for thirty years, Anne and I stayed on an island in Lake Temagami in northern Ontario as the guests of John Hyde, a former student and later colleague in the Williams history department. Cattle Island — presumably so named because Ojibway Indians had once tried unsuccessfully to raise some cows there — is about two miles from Bear Island, where the Hudson's Bay Company had established a fur-trading post in the 1870s, and later a post office and a convenience store, which have now been taken over by a "band" of the Ojibway Indians.

For many years John conducted ecumenical Protestant services in the Anglican Mission Church of St. George's on Bear Island. I sometimes assisted by reading the Scriptures. One Sunday morning, the assigned reading was the passage in the Gospel of St. Matthew in which Jesus speaks of feeding the hungry, clothing the naked, giving drink to the thirsty, visiting prisoners, and welcoming strangers.

Foolishly, I had failed to check the church's Bible ahead of time. When I arrived at the lectern I was horrified to see that half the page of Matthew, chapter 25, verses 35–36 had been torn out of the Bible. I tried desperately to remember the passage and found myself ad-libbing and repeating myself. The stolid Indians in the front row were not paying much attention, but when they found themselves being clothed, fed, welcomed, and visited for the third and fourth time, their interest picked up remarkably.

The accommodations on Cattle Island were comfortable but primitive. No plumbing, no telephone or TV, and no electricity. We bathed on one side of the island and drank water from the other side. We learned to regulate natural functions, since ninety-eight yards separated sleeping quarters from the two sanitary pit privies — known as the Upper and Lower Belvederes because each had been decorated with hand-carved totems.

Few conveniences, but days and nights beatified by glorious silence. We did not miss man-made noises. As we lay in bed at night we counted the sounds: loon couples serenading each other in any one of their eight distinct calls, a "moping owl which to the moon complained," poplar leaves rustled by gentle breezes, and "lake water lapping with low sounds on the shore."

One late August afternoon we spotted a black bear eating blueberries in our cove. That same warm evening, Anne, John, and I were reading in the living room when Anne excused herself to make the long trek to the Lower Belvedere. Chief, then our family sheltie, accompanied her. Suddenly, the stillness of the night was shattered by Anne's terrifying screams and the dog's frantic barking. "My God," I yelled, "the bear has got Anne!"

I grabbed an ax and John his power light and we started up the path. In the dim moonlight we could see Anne standing on one leg while kicking the other frantically and ineffectively. Her heartrending screams and cries of "No! No! No!" intermingled with the desperate barking of the circling dog.

As we approached with the light, we could see the cause of her terror: A large, slippery toad had been caught in the thong of her Japanese flip-flops. The more she kicked, the more it flopped and wound its cold and slimy self around her warm bare leg.

One way to get to Lake Temagami from Williamstown was to spend the night at a fishing camp in the settlement of Deux-Rivières in northern Ontario, about an hour from North Bay, where we would buy groceries for our stay on Cattle Island.

Since restaurant food in rural Ontario is notoriously awful, I asked Doug Antler, the genial proprietor of the fishing camp, where we could get a decent supper. He said that a friend of his had just taken over a café about two miles west on Highway 17, and the food was pretty good. The new name of the place was the Aftica Inn.

I found the name interesting. Since I knew that in the eighteenth century the convergence of the "two rivers" was a noted fur-trading area, I asked if the restaurant were named after an Indian tribe. I had not heard of the Aftica Indians. Doug said, "Hell, no! My friend named the place after his wife." He went on to say that his friend was a thoroughly happy-go-lucky guy whose wife was constantly urging him to be more ambitious, to try new adventures. She talked him into buying this run-down restaurant and completely refurbishing it to make it a going proposition. He finally yielded to his wife's entreaties but said he'd name it after her. He had a huge and expensive sign specially made with its new name — *The Aftica Inn.* It stands for "Another Fucking Thing I Can't Afford."

It is the only restaurant we know that we patronize because of its name and not its food.

After closing up the camp one September, we began thinking of alternative routes back to Williamstown. John suggested it might be fun for Anne and me to go home indirectly by stopping off at the village of Moosonee on James Bay, then visit Moose Factory, an island in James Bay where we would find a large Hudson's Bay post — one of the first on the North American continent — a school, a hospital, and the Anglican Cathedral, the seat of the Bishop of Moosonee.

We drove north as far as we could go to Cochrane, Ontario, where the highway swings west to cross Canada. We stayed that night in a small motel, where we left the car and the next day took the "Polar Bear Express," the small train that shuttles on the Ontario Northland railway between Cochrane and Moosonee. We were on the last run of the summer and were given two-inch-high plastic polar bears as souvenirs of the trip.

At Moosonee, Cree Indians took us in a fifteen-man canoe across the choppy, cold, rain-whipped water to Moose Factory. Upon landing, we were greeted by a sign reading "The Anglican Ladies of Moose Factory

Welcome You." An arrow directed us to enter a tepee. We took refuge from the rain in the tepee's cozy warmth, where pleasant-faced Indian women smiled a welcome and offered us bannock bread, which they were cooking over an open fire of sweet-smelling hardwood coals. Their recipe, they told us, had been handed down to them from their grandparents, who had received it from the Scots family who had established the original Bay trading post. The dough, which is a cross between that of a scone and a baking-powder biscuit and flavored with fresh blueberries, was wrapped around a green stick and rotated over the open fire, as one roasts wieners or marshmallows. Mugs of hot strong tea and the delicious bread warmed both our stomachs and what my father called the cockles of our hearts. (I never knew exactly what my cockles were.)

We paid our dollars, thanked the ladies and took the boardwalk to St. Thomas Cathedral, which must be unique in Christendom: the only one with six-inch holes bored through its floor. Hardwood plugs are pulled out every spring, we were told, in order to allow about two feet of water to seep into the nave to anchor the wooden church — it was said that a previous cathedral had floated away in the spring flood.

We returned to Cochrane, picked up our car, and headed home, driving diagonally across Quebec through La Verendrye Provincial Reserve. After passing hundreds of miles of spruce, pine, and tamarac, we stopped for the night in a spanking-new motel, the Mont Laurier.

Room number six contained a marvelous example of Canadian motel art. Painted in iridescent colors and with velvetlike texture, the picture contained almost every imaginable cliché: a mountain pool with a stag at eve standing beside palm trees, drinking his fill as a full moon shines brightly on the snows of Mt. Fujiyama. The picture, I thought, lacked only one thing: Next to one of the palm trees, I stuck our souvenir polar bear.

I simply had to find out how it had weathered the winter, so at the close of our following summer at Temagami, I rang up the Mont Laurier and reserved room number six. After the long trek, we arrived at the motel and hurried expectantly to our room. Some insensitive dolt had removed our bear.

DAVID FROST INTERVIEW WITH DAVID IRVING:
"Hitler Was Not an Anti-Semite"

One afternoon in 1977 I received a telephone call in my office at Williams from David Frost's secretary in London, asking me if I would be willing along with David Irving to appear on the TV show *David Frost Interviews.*

David Irving, a prolific right-wing writer, had recently published *Hitler's War,* a sensational book that among many other things argued that Hitler was not responsible for the Holocaust and had not known what was happening to the Jews. Irving is a showman who has taken to waving a 1,000-pound note in front of his audiences and offering it to anyone who can find a piece of paper signed by Hitler ordering the massacre of Jews. The secretary said that Mr. Frost thought that my appearance with Irving would make for a lively discussion. He was certainly right about that.

The telephone call had come on Friday afternoon; the show was to be aired the following Monday evening. As Frost's guests, could my wife and I fly on Saturday? I told her I would ring her back in ten minutes. I called Anne, asking if she could fly with me to London "tomorrow night." She said sure, her passport was valid; she'd wash her hair and be set to go. I reported acceptance.

We were booked into the BBC hotel. At the working lunch on Sunday, Mr. Frost, also the son of a Methodist pastor, greeted me: "Well, Professor Waite, I see that we have something in common. We're both PKs." I hadn't heard the expression since my childhood at Rock Lake.

"You know, of course,
that Hitler was not personally an anti-Semite."

I had brought to the luncheon a copy of my Hitler book with its colored photograph of the eerily dramatic portrait of the Führer. Frost was struck by it and commented, "I don't recall ever seeing that picture." I told him that I doubted that anyone in Great Britain had. He said, "Well, they will tomorrow night!"

On Monday evening, shortly before we were to appear on the show, I met Mr. Irving for the first time. He was a large, handsome, dark-haired man dressed impeccably in a Savile Row suit; he had been delivered to the studio in his chauffeur-driven Daimler. He had cold eyes and a smile that reminded me of Sir Robert Peel's: It was like the silver plate on a coffin. He treated me with contempt.

As soon as we were on the air, Irving turned to me and said, "Well, now, Professor Waite, you know, of course, that Hitler was not personally an anti-Semite."

I was stunned for a moment and then said that I felt as if I had come 2,900 miles to talk about Rembrandt and had been told at the outset, "Let us proceed with our discussion of Rembrandt by agreeing that he was not an artist."

The interview rapidly degenerated into a shouting match of which I am not proud. As an interview it was a shambles, but the twelve-foot-high colored photo of my book's cover, which served as a backdrop to the show, did not hurt sales in Britain.

After we were off the air, Irving told the studio audience that there was only one person in the room who really knew Hitler's true attitude to the Jews, and he asked a former personal SS adjutant to Hitler to stand up. This Stumpf-hyphen-von-Something arose and dutifully said that he had never known the Führer to say anything "unkindly" about Jews. I told Anne I thought I was going to be sick, and we left the room.

THE MAKING OF *KAISER AND FÜHRER*

M y memoirs up to this point have been largely anecdotal. This section will be different in content and tone, for I will be discussing problems and issues that I faced in writing my last book of serious scholarship, the culmination of my academic career. In the part dealing with similarities and differences between the two men — the central theme of my comparative study — I will give a fairly complete summary of some of my findings. Readers who are not interested in this discussion are cordially invited to skip these pages.

• • • • •

The book started in this way: After publishing my biography of Adolf Hitler in 1977, I had gone to Oxford for the first time in 1978 with the intention of beginning work on a biography of Kaiser Wilhelm II. I was particularly interested in examining the papers left to St. Antony's college by Sir John Wheeler-Bennett. I had heard a rumor that he was interested in writing about Wilhelm II because he himself was one of the Kaiser's illegitimate sons. Indeed, there really was a striking resemblance between him and August-Wilhelm, the Kaiser's youngest son, who became a member of Hitler's Brown Shirts and a rabid Nazi. This resemblance was deeply embarrassing to Wheeler-Bennett. When he visited Germany in the 1930s, he was frequently and obsequiously addressed as *Kaiserliche Hoheit* (Imperial Majesty). Although the resemblance was uncanny, the rumor had no basis in fact, even though it was repeated to me by no less a person than Lord Alan Bullock, the distinguished European historian. And it was believed for a time by Winston Churchill. Wheeler-Bennett himself flatly denied the story: "My dear mother had never even met a Hohenzollern in her life."

I became intrigued with the complex — indeed baffling — character of Wilhelm II and thought of writing a full-length biography that would parallel my study of the connection between Hitler's psychopathology and his politics.

But I soon found out that that had already occurred to several other historians, people who were more experienced in Wilhelmian studies than I, and several of them were already completing full-length biographies of the Kaiser. These historians included my successor in German history at Williams College, the extraordinarily gifted Thomas A. Kohut, trained in both psychopathology and history, who was then at work revising his doctoral thesis concerned with the way Wilhelm's psychopathology affected his appeal to the German people. (In 1991 Oxford Press would publish his impressive study, *Wilhelm II and the Germans: A Study of Leadership*.)

While conversing over lunch one day in the Buttery at St. Antony's College, Antony Nicholls, senior tutor in history, suggested that I might "lead from strength," drawing on my knowledge of Hitler's personality to write a book about both men, a comparison of the Kaiser and the Führer. I liked the idea and spent the next twenty years working on it.

"Man or Circumstance?"

The book challenged me because it forced me to come to grips with several basic historical problems I had been thinking about for fifty years of teaching and writing history.

For example, in determining the course of history, how decisive is the role played by individual personality when compared with the force of external circumstance?

Historians who argue the importance of personality take comfort from Thomas Carlyle's conclusion that "history is but the essence of innumerable biographies." The same idea was recently expressed by a British writer looking back over the present century: "The political history of the twentieth century," he said, "can be written as the biographies of seven men: Lenin, Stalin, Hitler, Mao Tse-tung, Gandhi, Franklin Roosevelt, and Winston Churchill." The list of great names over the centuries can easily be expanded. Jesus, Charlemagne, Marx, William the Conqueror, Gutenberg, Napoleon, Freud, Copernicus, Einstein, and Mandela remind us that individual lives have changed the course of history.

Other historians see the matter differently. Those who stress the importance of circumstance insist that nonpersonal forces such as governmental structure, social conditions, and economic forces determine historical development. Marxists, for example, are not impressed with biography. I recall a luncheon with two colleagues who were doing research at the *Institut für Zeitgeschichte* during my second sabbatical in Munich: a Soviet scholar who was working on a "new history of modern Germany," Richard M. Hunt, now the Marshal of Harvard University, who was then studying the career of Joseph Goebbels for his doctoral dissertation, and myself, who was working on Hitler.

When Rick Hunt complimented the Russian on his ambitious project, the Soviet scholar asked him when he expected to finish his study of Goebbels and was amazed when Hunt told him "in about five more years." He then turned to me and asked when I would finish my book on Hitler. I said I had been working on the Führer for about five years and hoped to finish in another ten. He simply could not believe it: "Fifteen years on *one person?* It's not possible! Why do you waste so much time on one man? No individual is worth that much time! Certainly not when compared with the *really decisive* part played by economic forces!" When I asked when he hoped to complete his new history of modern Germany, he said, "In about a year," and added, "You see, I already know what happened and the kind of evidence I am looking for."

Historians of Germany who have been called "structuralists" also downplay the importance of such individuals as Wilhelm II and Hitler. The governments of the Second and Third Reichs, they insist, were run not by the Kaiser and the Führer but by the internal dynamics of impersonal structures: governmental, military, and economic forces. There was no "personal rule" by the Kaiser, for Wilhelm was merely an ineffective figurehead constantly pushed about by forces and circumstances he was not strong enough to control.

A similar case was made about Hitler's Germany at an international conference I attended at Harvard in 1983 to mark the fiftieth anniversary of Hitler's "seizure of power." Valuable papers were given on new discoveries that had been made during the past half century about such topics as the careers of women, the role of the medical doctors and judges, and the everyday life of average citizens in the Third Reich.

All were worthwhile. But when I realized that no one had been invited to present a paper on Adolf Hitler, this fact struck me — as I have said — not unlike staging *Hamlet* without the Melancholy Dane.

I don't remember even hearing the word "Hitler" spoken until the second day of the conference, when Professor Hans Mommsen, a noted

German structuralist, was reporting on his research on the Nazi bureaucracy. In an aside, he repeated the phrase he had previously used in several valuable, if combative, scholarly articles in which he argued that because "Hitler was actually a weak dictator," it was professional civil servants who actually ran the Third Reich.

Structuralist research in institutional history has made valuable contributions to our knowledge of how the governments of both the Second and the Third Reich actually operated. Yet, in my view, this has not displaced the Kaiser or the Führer as dominating forces of their governments.

I believe that personality and circumstance are both essential to our understanding of history. To choose one and not the other is like trying to construct water with either hydrogen or oxygen alone.

In about the year 438 B.C., Herodotus struggled with the problem of the causes of the wars between Persia and Greece. He concluded, according to one translation, "Methinks the Causes of these Wars lie in the Interplay of Man and Circumstance."

Methinks the same principle applies to the Second and Third German Reichs.

"CHANGE OR CONTINUITY?"
AND A HARVARD SEMINAR

In writing about the Kaiser and the Führer I was confronted by another problem that intrigues historians: Is the course of history determined more by change or by continuity?

It is an old problem. When our parents took a freshman history course in college, many of them were taught by advocates of change who believed that the Middle Ages — or sometimes the Dark Ages — was a culturally stagnant period between two golden ages. After the great period of Greece and Rome, it was confidently asserted, the Western world had fallen into a deep sleep until it suddenly awakened in the bright daylight of the Italian Renaissance of the fifteenth century. My undergraduate courses changed that impression. We were assigned Charles Homer Haskins's classic *The Renaissance of the Twelfth Century,* and new studies of the "Carolingian Renaissance" under Charlemagne also emphasized the essential continuity of European intellectual and cultural history.

This question becomes acute in any discussion of the connection between the two German rulers. The argument for continuity was made most clearly in William L. Shirer's immensely popular book, *The Rise and Fall of the Third Reich,* probably the most influential book that has ever been written on German history. Shirer saw a direct connection between the Second Reich of Wilhelm II and the Third Reich of Adolf Hitler:

Nazism was but a logical continuation of German history . . . From 1871 to 1933 and indeed until Hitler's end in 1945, the course of

> *German history . . . was to run, with the exception of the interim of the Weimar Republic . . . in a straight line and with utter logic.*

Proponents of change were quick to lambaste Shirer's book as a simplistic version of German history that was not, as one critic bitterly wrote, "a tortured prologue to Hitler's Reich." The barbarous ethos, the tone and purpose of Hitler's state, he insisted, was a world apart from the Kaiser's civilized Germany.

I agree with the well-worn observation that "the past determines the present." For I believe it is true that in the life of individuals, as in the life of nations, our present is indeed heavily influenced by what happened in the past. But I would also suggest that *the present may determine our past* — at least our view of the past.

I remember defending that proposition during a discussion at Harvard when Richard Hunt, a friend since our year together at the *Institut für Zeitgeschichte* in Munich, had asked me to talk about my Hitler book, which he had assigned to his seminar in historical biography. It was a joy to visit again with Rick and Priscilla, his delightful wife, to stay overnight in their lovely old home on Coolidge Hill Road, and to sleep in the bed that had given rest to Chancellor Helmut Kohl's 296 pounds as well as other notable bodies — all of whom had been Rick's guests in his capacity as marshal of the university.

During the seminar discussion, a student had argued for continuity and asked me if I didn't think that, given Germany's history, it was "just in the cards that Hitler would come to power." I suggested to the student that the answer to his question depended heavily on the historical perspective of the person writing the history. I, for example, had written my book with the knowledge that Hitler had come to power and established his malevolent dictatorship during my historical present. Certainly Hitler had been helped by aspects of Germany's history: habits of deference and obedience to "the authorities," pernicious traditions of aggressive militarism, a persistent siren call through the centuries for a powerful Führer, a new Barbarossa, and by German domination of central Europe and a desire to avenge the hated *Versailles-Diktat.* Further,

Hitler's vicious racism was helped by the fact that for centuries obsessive hatred and fear of Jews had been expressed by Germany's most influential religious and secular leaders: Martin Luther, Johann Fichte, Immanuel Kant, Artur Schopenhauer, Heinrich von Treitschke, Richard Wagner, among many others.

All that is true. But what if my historical present had been different? What if Adolf Hitler, on trial for treason against the Weimar Republic in the spring of 1924, had been found guilty — as the evidence clearly dictated — and had been deported to his native Austria — as the law required?

What if the "interim of the Weimar Republic" had been prolonged and, commencing in 1924 with the stabilization of the German mark and many other hopeful signs, democracy and not dictatorship had taken root in the Fatherland?

If that had happened, I would have written no book on Adolf Hitler; instead, I might have written on the triumph of Germany's first experiment with democracy and looked to the past to find its historical roots. I could have found many of those roots in the Kaiser's Reich, with its respect for law, where diverse opinions were expressed in a full range of newspapers and periodicals, where there was a freely elected parliament, comprehensive social legislation, and a high degree of personal liberty, and where creative ideas and solid achievement enhanced every field of human endeavor: in philosophy, theology, science, and medicine, as well as in literature, theater, music, art, and architecture.

If Germany's first experiment in democracy had succeeded, my discussion of Germany's history would have been very different. But I was not confronted with a healthy democracy; I was confronted with Hitler's vicious dictatorship, and I sought to explain its origins.

Objectivity, Sincerity, and the Historian

In graduate school I once met an intense and humorless young man who insisted that history was quite correctly seen as "social science" and quoted a famous British historian who had proclaimed that "history is science . . . nothing more and nothing else." That is why, the young man continued, we historians must be rigorously objective, dispassionate, and morally neutral. We must eschew all "value judgments."

I did not tell him that I thought he was full of Brussels sprouts.

Historians are not scientists. We do not deal with inert molecules and morally neutral sulfuric acids; we deal with human beings of flesh and blood, emotions and psyches, who do things that we judge to be noble and evil, capricious and calculated, generous and despicable. And we should label their actions as such.

In writing about Wilhelm Hohenzollern and Adolf Hitler, I had no desire to be morally neutral; I did strive to be fair-minded. And I certainly made "value judgments." For in my view, the task of the historian is not merely to record the past; it is to interpret the past, and that requires judgment.

Let us be clear about "objectivity." When the word is associated with intellectual integrity, it is good; both our conscience and our craft tell us not to distort facts in order to fit our subjective interpretations. But when "objective" is made synonymous with moral neutrality, it is not good. Indeed, I believe that it is neither possible nor desirable for historians to be morally neutral.

How can any historian remain indifferent to the way the United States Army massacred American Indians and Vietnamese civilians? Are we to withhold personal judgment about Allied decisions, during the last stages of the war, to fire-bomb the lovely baroque cities of Dresden and Würzburg, whose military importance was negligible? Are we to remain "completely objective" about Auschwitz?

In my view, to assume such a stance would be to abjure informed judgment and, in so doing, to abandon our responsibility as historians. After studying the careers of Kaiser and Führer, I felt obliged to pass judgment on those careers.

Some of the problems associated with historical objectivity were brought home to me in the classroom. In a freshman course in European history, during a discussion of Nazi concentration camps, I read aloud from the testimony presented at the Nuremberg Trials and from the horrendous diaries of concentration-camp victims. After class, a pretty freshman coed with brightly brushed hair and an engaging smile said, "That was very interesting, sir. But I thought it was a little one-sided. It really wasn't objective at all. Your evidence all came from one point of view. Don't you think we should hear what Hitler and other Nazis said about those camps? We really ought to consider the other side, shouldn't we, sir?" Yes, I said, let us consider the Nazi side of the matter. It was well expressed by Hitler when he said, "Jews should be treated like vermin . . . like vermin, they will be exterminated." You are right, Miss Thompson, there are indeed two sides of this issue; one of them is revolting. The victims of evil are not to be balanced off by the perpetrators of evil.

About a week later a young man, who happened to come from Minneapolis, was writing an essay on Heinrich Himmler and the SS. He came to my office and in the process of discussing his research said, "You know, sir, you really have to give Himmler credit: He was sincere." I said I agreed and that we could also give him credit for being no hypocrite.

But, I continued, as one might say in Minnesota, "That is yust the hahll of it!" The horrors of history have been committed not by hypocrites — not by the Uriah Heeps and the Tartuffes — but by fanatically sincere men like Torquemada, Robespierre, Pol Pot, and Himmler. Sincere and devout men like Hitler, who, in murdering Jews, said that he was "doing the work of the Lord." A sincerely motivated act is not necessarily a good act. Rapists and bank robbers are usually sincere.

Moreover, as my friend Fred Stocking has pointed out, a case can be made for a little wholesome insincerity. Good manners and civility may be more appropriate than sincerity. Suppose I am walking down Spring Street one fine spring day and I see approaching a person whose guts I hate, as I am confident he hates mine. As we meet we wish each other "Good morning!" Both statements are insincere, and both are hypocritical. But both show better judgment than impolite sincerity that could have ruined a lovely morning by precipitating a messy scene.

Sincerity is not necessarily a virtue. I will not be impressed with your sincerity, Mr. Anderson, until I know what you are sincere about. Tell me not that you are sincere. Very sincere men in power can frighten the hell out of me.

"What Actually Happened"

I confronted another historical issue when I reexamined the great Leopold von Ranke's famous phrase about the purpose of history. "Our task," he said, "is simply to find out what actually happened." That is, find the facts.

That is certainly a worthy objective, but it does not go far enough. For often it is more important to find out what people *believed* to have happened. For in history, as in personal lives, *belief* about what happened may be more compelling than the truth.

Marie Antoinette, for instance, probably did not dismiss the hungry mothers of France who had marched from Paris to Versailles pleading for bread with the comment, "If they have no bread, let them eat cake." But the French masses believed she had said it, and that belief reinforced their picture of the French queen as a callous, frivolous "foreigner" who treated common people with contempt. Nor was the rumor true that she had oral sex with her eleven-year-old son, the Dauphin of France. But, again, that rumor was believed and the belief fueled the fires of hatred against the "Austrian bitch" and, hence, the French monarchy.

In November 1918 the German army was defeated in the field; it was not "stabbed in the back" by "traitorous socialists and Jews of the Weimar Republic." That fact of military defeat is demonstrable, but it is not so important to the future as the fact that thousands of German patriots *believed* the stab-in-the-back legend and their erroneous belief engendered hatred of the new democracy.

With regard to Hitler, we will probably never know whether his grandfather was in fact a Jew. But the more important fact is that Hitler believed *he might have been,* and this devastating fear that he himself might be "part Jewish" haunted him throughout his life and shaped history.

He expressed his fear of that direct threat to his personal identity and his political life in a number of ways. As soon as he had conquered Austria, he gave orders that the cemetery in the little Austrian village where his grandparents were buried was to be used as a *Wehrmacht* artillery target, thus obliterating the gravestones of his ancestors.

On three separate occasions he ordered his SS to investigate his ancestors in order to prove that he had not one drop of "Jewish blood." The SS were unable to find that proof. Hitler therefore sought ways to invent "proof."

One way was to become history's greatest scourge of the Jews. In effect he was saying, "See, I cannot possibly be part Jewish. I'll *prove it to you* [and to myself]. I'll kill the Jews," and screaming that he would "annihilate the Jews down to the third generation" — that is, down to the degree of blood relationship he was so desperately trying to prove could not possibly be his own.

Hitler tried, as psychologists would say, "to externalize and project" his hatred and fear of the Jews, but he never managed to do so. Many revealing phrases indicate that he felt Jewishness to be *an evil within himself,* a demon to be exorcised. During a private conversation he reviewed the ways he had attacked the Jews but finally despaired of ever being rid of them. The Jew, Hitler said, "is an invisible demon" that can never be ultimately eradicated because, he concluded bitterly, "the Jew is always within us" *(Der Jude sitzt immer in uns).*

What Hitler believed to be true about his personal past had dreadful consequences for the future.

SIMILARITIES AND DIFFERENCES

The idea of writing a comparative study of Kaiser and Führer appealed to me, for I could see both marked similarities and striking differences between the two German rulers.

I noted that both Wilhelm and Hitler were deeply disturbed mentally and in both rulers psychopathology was politically helpful. Both were adored by the German people, especially by women. Both led their countries to ruin and the world to war. Both were born with physical defects that they blamed on their mother, the Kaiser with a withered left arm, the Führer with a missing left testicle. Both wrote poetry and painted quite acceptable watercolors. Both were cruel yet kind, cowardly yet brave, creative yet destructive. Both rulers remained childlike: The favorite game of the Emperor of Germany was tag. Screaming with laughter, he chased his guests around the royal yacht. The Führer liked to see how fast he could get undressed and jump into bed. Both preached sermons and ordered the deaths of millions of innocent people. Both were anti-Semites, the Kaiser preceding the Führer when he said in 1919, "The best way would be gas." Both were indicted as war criminals.

Yet there were also striking differences. Wilhelm was "to the purple born," his future was assured; as the heir to the Hohenzollern throne, he was destined to rule his nation. Hitler was born in obscurity; a school dropout, he clawed his uncertain way through flophouses, beer halls, and back alleys to become ruler of Germany and, for a season, arbiter of Europe.

I discovered that both men had been battered as children. I already knew about Adolf. The testimony of Hitler's neighbors in the little

Austrian village of Leonding, where Hitler spent much of his childhood, along with interviews with his sister, Paula, and his half brother, made it clear that Adolf had been brutally whipped "every day" by their sadistic father, Alois Hitler, who also brutalized Adolf's mother. Even old Josef Mayrhofer, the mayor of the village and Herr Hitler's *Stammtisch* crony admitted that Alois was "damn rough" at home and that his wife and children had "nothing to smile about." He also remembered that the Hitler children were ordered to use the formal *"Sie"* in talking to their father and to address him as *"Herr Vater."*

In reading the "Dear Mama" letters of Wilhelm's mother to Queen Victoria in the Royal Archives in Windsor Castle, I was surprised to learn that she, too, had in fact brutalized her infant son in her well-meant but hopeless and cruel efforts to "cure" his incurable birth injury.

The motivations of the parents were vastly different. Adolf was brutalized by a viciously sadistic father who howled with laughter as he beat his son with his dog whip; Willie was tortured by a loving and well-meaning mother who was trying to help him. But how was Willie to know that? What he knew was that his mother forced him to use his useless arm, tried to straighten his deformed shoulder by cranking it in a machine, and supervised electrical shocks that tore through his body. She then showered him with kisses and tearful protestations of her love. The kid was confused.

There was another difference in their childhood experiences. Willie Hohenzollern could always find love, comfort, and understanding from his two favorite grandparents, his maternal grandmother, Queen Victoria, who adored her favorite grandchild, and his beloved paternal grandfather, old King-Emperor Wilhelm I, who took his favorite grandson on his lap and told him exciting stories about his military exploits in Prussia's victorious wars.

Little Dolfie Hitler had no such refuge. There was no one he could turn to — not his mother, Klara, who was as terrified as he was by her brutal husband; not his grandparents, whom Hitler never mentioned.

The atmospheres of the childhood homes were different. Wilhelm enjoyed the amenities of a royal household, as well as the security he must have felt from parents who loved him and each other. They provided him with an excellent education. His first language was English, which he spoke with his mother and grandmother, then German with his father and grandfather. His French tutor said that his French was *"impeccable,"* a judgment borne out by the many French exercise books I found in the ex-Kaiser's library in Doorn House. As his library shows, he kept up his use of languages by reading in the originals the great classics of French, English, German, and Italian literature and philosophy. His mother broke with tradition by sending her firstborn to a good *Gymnasium,* where he learned the Latin he liked to quote throughout his life. He attended Bonn University, where he read law and political economy.

Hitler's boyhood home crackled with tension and terror and the unpredictable rages of *Herr Vater.* His mother, who was illiterate, could not help him with his education. The only language he knew was German, and that imperfectly. He received D and D-minus marks in German in elementary school and never completed high school. He wrote *Mein Kampf,* the book that made him a millionaire, but as a sedulous German critic has counted, it contained 1,200 mistakes in German grammar and syntax. Although Hitler knew no language other than German, he felt confident when making such pronouncements as "Anybody can master French in three weeks" and "Nowhere is Shakespeare so badly acted as in England." He possessed a private library of some 5,000 books, collected largely, I suspect, to impress fellow Nazis with his erudition. As one of his secretaries said in an interview, "In it there was not one book of lasting humane or intellectual value."

Women found both Kaiser and Führer attractive. But Hitler's appeal was more intense and certainly more bizarre.

In 1953 when I visited Munich's famous *Hofbräuhaus,* an elderly hatcheck woman told me that she and her colleagues had always looked forward to one of Hitler's speeches in the giant *Schweme* because dozens of women would tip her extravagantly for letting them kiss the sweatband of the Führer's hat.

Hitler had four attractive and intelligent secretaries. None of them was married. When the prettily charming Gerda Christian was asked why neither she nor any of her colleagues had married, she replied, "How could any of us marry after having known Adolf Hitler?"

After the war an American officer found, in the ruins of Hitler's Reichschancellery, a cache of some 800 letters marked "Love Letters to the Führer." They were written by women of all walks of life, each of whom was convinced that she alone was the Führer's one true love. All of them used the familiar *"du"* and tried to express the fervor of their love by inventing endearing and often almost untranslatable diminutives: "My own true heart and sweet little Dolfy" . . . "My own hottest sweetest lover and mighty Führer" . . . "My very own heartthrob."

One woman wrote that she had sold her family home in Vienna and taken a room in war-ravaged Berlin just to be near her lover. She enclosed two keys: one to the rooming house, one to her private room. Many of the women promised Hitler "the hottest sex" — oral or any kind he would like. One woman wrote that she could understand if Hitler was too busy to sleep with her but begged him to send her some of his precious semen so that she could fulfill "the sole purpose of my life" — to bear the Führer's son.

Kaiser and Führer both loved to keep their entourage up late at night talking. Both were compelling speakers who could rouse audiences to a high emotional pitch. But there were great differences.

Wilhelm's conversations were nuanced and knowledgeable. He enjoyed vigorous intellectual debate on an impressive variety of subjects about which he was well informed. He liked being with intellectuals, discussing novels and philosophy with professors, counterpoint with Cosima Wagner, technical aspects of ship construction and maintenance with Albert Ballin, participating actively in the seminars on cultural anthropology and archaeology that he sponsored in Doorn.

Hitler despised intellectuals and was frightened by them. With the exception of Albert Speer, he surrounded himself with people whose minds were as rigid, coarse, and cruel as his own. He did not debate with anyone; indeed, he did not really converse, he harangued captive audiences about the same shallow and fetid subjects interminably, hour after hour, and pontificated about subjects about which he was uninformed:

"In the single year 1641, 50,000 Irish left for North America . . . You can't imagine anything as degenerate as American farmers . . . The English language is incapable of expressing a poetic idea . . . Russia has never suffered a famine . . . Czechs were originally Mongolians . . . No one in the Middle Ages suffered from high blood pressure."

A secretary who had survived a hundred nights of Hitler's verbal barrages reflected, "His spate of words lacked the human note, the spiritual quality of a cultivated man . . . There was nothing on which the human spirit had left its trace."

The Kaiser's major speeches were carefully prepared and replete with well-turned phrases, fresh metaphors, and nuanced argument. The Führer's bombast simply repeated, in exactly the same phrases, the same poisonous ideas. The speeches of 1920 are virtually identical with those of 1944.

There was another major difference in their spoken words. The Kaiser was sometimes carried away by his own rhetoric, said things he really did not mean, and was not taken seriously by governmental officials. When he ordered the army to "shoot down like mad dogs" the workers who went on strike, or during the war to "starve to death" all Russian prisoners of war, German officials assumed he did not want to be obeyed.

The hell of Hitler was that he meant what he said and he practiced what he preached. When he said he wanted all the Jews of the Greater German Reich "utterly annihilated," he was obeyed. He kept his promises — at least some of them. As Elie Wiesel noted with bitter irony, he was the only one who kept his promises to the Jewish people.

Both Kaiser and Führer claimed to speak for the German people and to identify with them. Wilhelm liked to see himself as "the people's Kaiser." But for him it was a romantic notion, a rhetorical flourish, a role he enjoyed playing. More often it was belied by other public statements. He announced that he couldn't care less about his popularity or the opinions of the common people. He composed a little ditty he enjoyed quoting on inappropriate occasions:

Ich schau herab von meinem Tier
Auf das Gehudel unter mir.

(Mounted high in my saddle,
I glance beneath me at the rabble.)

Wilhelm was a social snob whose veins were full of royal blood. Adolf Hitler was a man of the masses, *Kleinbürger* incarnate, whose taste in art and literature was banal, whose speeches were larded with hackneyed patriotic clichés and common grammatical errors, and whose very stylistic mediocrity had wide appeal. He did not so much "conquer the masses" as identify with them.

But though he was one of the masses, he was set apart from them by a touch of political genius. None of Hitler's political competitors showed a remotely comparable ability to sense the psychic needs of his audiences and to demonstrate that he was one of them: He, too, had been a common laborer and a common soldier; he, too, had known hunger and privation. He was proud to be one of the common people: "When I speak to you today, and thus to millions of others, I have more right to do this than anyone else. I have grown out of you . . . I was among you in the war for four and a half years . . . in my youth I was a worker like you."

And again his words flew like an arrow to their hearts: "I am so happy to live among this people and so proud to be permitted to be called your Leader — so proud that I cannot imagine anything in this world that I would rather be. I should a thousand times rather be the lowest *Volksgenosse* (racial comrade) among you than a king anywhere else . . . I have fought for this *Volk,* I will continue to fight for this *Volk* and for this *Volk* I would let myself be hacked to pieces!"

There was a revealing difference between the ways in which Kaiser and Führer cast their speeches. Wilhelm did not expect audiences to participate; he expected the respectful applause that was his royal due. Hitler encouraged audience participation, leaving spaces in his speeches for the crowds to scream, *Sieg Heil! Ein Volk! Ein Reich! Ein Führer!* The Führer himself sometimes got carried away and joined in the frenzied chorus.

As rulers of Germany, both men displayed remarkable political ability along with monumental stupidity.

The Kaiser's political performance was erratic to the extreme. Like the little girl with the curl in the middle of her forehead, when he was good he was very good; when he was bad he was appalling.

He showed impressive skill in building the Imperial German Navy. He knew that such a vast program would need broad support from the entire population and the German parliament. He made the most successful appointment of his reign in the extraordinarily dedicated, energetic and gifted Admiral Alfred Tirpitz.

He encouraged the formation of such interest groups as the Naval League to put pressure on the Reichstag; he made dozens of passionate speeches throughout the Reich; he prefabricated stories "to educate the masses" on the need for a mighty navy, and these were sent to every hometown newspaper in Germany; he inundated the Reich with thousands of broadsides and pamphlets; patriotic professors were enlisted to beat the drums of nationalism and naval power; pep rallies were held throughout Germany featuring fervent speeches and group singing of patriotic songs.

This calculated campaign to create a national *Marineschwärmerei* (naval craze) was successful. The Reichstag overwhelmingly passed massive naval bills that launched a naval race with Britain that became a contributing cause of the First World War.

His methods also set an important — and ominous — precedent: They were the starting point of the modern era of propaganda, by which the masses are mobilized and fanaticized in support of government policy — using techniques Hitler would bring to diabolical perfection.

Wilhelm also showed great political skill in his firm and sensible response to a threat of a military-rightist coup d'état in 1913. The Imperial Army, patriotic societies, and the extreme right had become increasingly alarmed by the growth of social democracy. They plotted a "coup from above" by which the Kaiser would order the army to dissolve the Reichstag, rule by decree, muzzle the press, confiscate Jewish property, and drive the Jews out of Germany. The conspirators enlisted the

Crown Prince — always a supporter of right-wing causes; years later he would join the Nazis — in their cause. He supported their plan with enthusiasm and sent a copy of their program to his father with a covering note urging him to adopt it.

The Kaiser answered his son in a blistering note, saying, "Coups might be acceptable in Latin America, but they are not, thank God, our practice in Germany." To muzzle the press was "stupid and dangerous," for in a modern state a free press serves as "an indispensable safety valve." The idea of punishing Jews and driving them out of Germany was equally stupid. "It would be an economic and cultural disaster. It would set us back 100 years and exclude us from the ranks of cultured nations."

But Wilhelm could also be remarkably inept. He had a penchant for alienating the influential people who wanted to help him. In his sensible letter to his son he spoke of the value of a free press as a safety valve; he also knew how valuable the press could be in helping get his programs enacted. Yet he reacted to mild criticism with a torrent of abuse that alienated influential journalists, calling them "liars and traitors" and announcing that "the stupid, pig-brained press should shut their yaps."

In Prussia-Germany the ruler obviously needed the approval of the army. Yet Wilhelm told his generals that compared with his grandfather, they were "a bunch of pygmies." He also tried to undertake a complete reform of the army without consulting his Chancellor, who was at that time a general officer. When he lost at one of his incessant games of skat, he said his opponents, two full generals, were "cheats."

The diplomatic corps could be useful if he were to carry out his ambitious foreign policy. Yet he told the Italian ambassador, "Next to the French, the people I hate worst are my diplomats," and he announced that "the entire diplomatic corps stinks of shit" *(Scheiss)*. It was one of his favorite words.

The biggest blunders of his reign took place during two interviews in 1908, one with a British colonel, the other with an American journalist. Wilhelm had sought to impress them with his command of foreign affairs and his skill as a diplomat. If he had deliberately planned simultaneously to alarm and antagonize his own countrymen, the French,

Italians, Russians, Japanese, and the British people, it would be difficult to imagine a greater success.

Adolf Hitler showed a similar pattern of brilliant political moves and disastrous failures.

The Führer was both a fanatical ideologue and a cunning opportunist. His skill as a political tactician is shown in the adroit way he wooed and won capitalists, Christians, and conservatives, many of whom had been put off by the radicalism of his "socialism" and the barbarity of his Brown Shirts.

He assured captains of industry that they were indispensable to his plans for the economic recovery of Germany; that he was not opposed to their "creative capitalism," only to "Jewish finance capitalism"; that he would defend their interests against the menace of communism and the "stultifying egalitarianism of democracy"; and that he put his faith in "creative individuality in both politics and economics."

He won over the army by promising to rearm Germany and avenge the shameful armistice and the *"Versailles-Diktat."* When generals became alarmed by the boasts of Hitler's Brown Shirts that they would take over the German army, Hitler massacred his own supporters in the "Blood Purge" of 1934.

Hitler could not have come to power without the approval of big industry and the conservatives who dominated the army. Nor could he have done it without the support of the Christian Church. Here, too, his technique was masterful. He ordered racist hotheads within his party (who had wanted to establish a de-Christianized neo-pagan Nazi "Church") to stop their effusions, and he startled them by announcing that Nazism was "actually Christian" *(tatsächlich christlich);* he gave orders that henceforth the Nazis were to appear as champions of public morality and family values, defenders of Christianity and the last bulwark against "atheistic communism." He ordered his Brown Shirts to shave, put on clean uniforms, and go to church every Sunday. Pleasantly surprised parishioners were impressed with their impeccable behavior. He filled his speeches with quotations from Jesus.

These devices were effective. From 1932 on, Christians became enthusiastic supporters of Adolf Hitler.

Hitler's first bid for political power in the famous Munich Beer Hall Putsch of November 1923 presaged his future performance by showing him capable of both remarkable ineptitude and extraordinary skill as a political leader.

He had promised not only to seize power in Bavaria but to march on Berlin to overthrow the Republic. Explicitly promising a new German national government, he announced to cheering followers that his purpose would be fulfilled "only when the black-white-red-swastika banner floats over the *Berliner Schloss*." Yet Hitler made no effort to win the support of the two military leaders whose support for such an undertaking was absolutely essential: General Hans von Seekt, commander of the national army, and General Eric Ludendorff, prestigious spokesman of nationalist, racist causes. Hitler's newspaper, the *Völkischer Beobachter,* gratuitously insulted Seekt, calling him a tool of a "Masonic conspiracy," and libeled his Jewish wife. Prior to the actual night of the *Putsch,* Hitler had failed even to inform Ludendorff about his plans.

Nor had he tried to win the support or neutrality of local military and civilian authorities who were indispensable to the success of his venture.

Preparations for a national revolution were grossly inadequate within Munich. Outside the city they were nonexistent. SA commanders in the north who were itching to overthrow the "Weimar Traitors" were not informed, nor were their Bavarian colleagues.

The night of the coup, Hitler entered the *Bürgerbräukeller* dressed in an ill-fitting morning coat. Cutting a ridiculous figure, he jumped onto a table, fired two pistol shots into the ceiling and announced that "The national revolution has taken place!" Then he gave an impassioned and largely irrelevant speech. An eyewitness later recalled thinking that he didn't look at all like a heroic leader: "Why, that poor little waiter!" *(armes Kellnerlein).*

The first eight or ten hours of any attempt at a coup are crucial. When it was imperative for Hitler to act quickly and decisively, he gave no orders at all. He made no effort to do the obvious: seize the telephone exchange, telegraph and radio stations, transport facilities, police headquarters, government buildings. The march next day was not Hitler's idea. It was apparently ordered by General Ludendorff, who was fed up with Hitler's uncertain dithering and incomprehensible behavior. No one knew where the march was going; in fact, no one had known from the start.

When the marchers encountered the Munich police, Hitler lay down to escape gunfire, then ran away and hid in Putzi Hanfstaengl's summer home, where, on 11 November, he surrendered to the Bavarian police.

A disgusted follower, tough veteran of the Great War and a dozen street battles on Hitler's behalf, spoke for many of his fellows: "Hitler led his men into battle with absolutely no protection. Then when things got tough, Adolf the Crazy Swell-Head *(der grössenwahnsinnige Adolf)* took off . . . and left his men in the lurch. *Revolution mit dem Maul!* Did you expect he'd do anything else?"

Arrested, imprisoned, charged with conspiracy and treason, and threatened with deportation back to Austria, Hitler, everyone assumed, was finished. Only a miracle could save him. The miracle was the brilliantly shrewd way Hitler used his trial for high treason in late February and March 1924.

He was in command all the way. As the transcript shows, he kept interrupting and haranguing government witnesses so loudly that the judge repeatedly asked him, deferentially, if he could not perhaps lower his voice.

His final plea was a masterpiece of invective, serving as a harbinger of orations to come. He began the most important speech of his career by defiantly accepting full responsibility for his attempt to overthrow the Republic:

> *I alone bear responsibility, but I am not a criminal because of that. If I stand here as a revolutionary it is a revolutionary against the (so-called) revolution. There is no such thing as high treason against the traitors of 1918.*

Hitler put the government of the Republic in the dock, accusing President Ebert, Chancellor Scheidemann, and all their "lackeys" of high treason against Germany.

At the close of the trial, thousands of his supporters jammed in front of the Ministry of Justice. In a preview of coming years, they kept screaming *Heil Hitler! Heil Hitler! Heil Hitler!* until he appeared on the balcony to accept their homage.

The Kaiser, living in exile, followed the trial closely and was impressed with Hitler's performance, writing in the margin of one of the newspapers I read in Doorn House, "Hitler is a true patriot, fighting to restore German honor."

Overnight the obscure Munich street agitator had become a national hero and martyr to the cause of a resurgent Germany. In the months after his release from his few comfortable months of detainment, where he dictated the book that was to make him wealthy, he reasserted himself as undisputed Führer of his scattered and distraught party, pulling it together and leading it to power within ten years. It was a feat rarely matched in history.

He had converted fiasco into triumph.

OPERATION BARBAROSSA:
"The World Will Hold Its Breath"

Hitler made many bad decisions during the Second World War. Two of the worst were his unprovoked attack on Russia, "Operation Barbarossa," and his sudden declaration of war against the United States.

By June 1941 Hitler was master of the European continent. But instead of consolidating his vast "Greater German Reich" and concentrating his forces against his only remaining foe, an isolated and desperately wounded England, he attacked the USSR, proclaiming that "the world will hold its breath." This he did at the time Stalin, whom he greatly admired, was his most valuable ally, shipping him thousands of tons of vital war supplies — iron ore, chrome, as well as oil, wheat, platinum, rubber, and timber.

One of the most astonishing pictures I can imagine in all military history shows Hitler's soldiers marching eastward into Russia on the morning of 22 June 1941 and staring in amazement as they watch Soviet freight trains traveling westward loaded with supplies for their army. There is no evidence that the Red Army, vitally weakened by Stalin's recent and draconian purges, was about to attack him.

Military historians have pointed out many of Hitler's blunders and missed opportunities during "Operation Barbarossa," and one asks the inevitable question: "What could possibly be going on in the head of this man?"

The question needs to be broadened beyond Hitler's specific tactical and strategic mistakes. The decision to wage war on Russia was in itself a colossal error. Consider the risk he was taking in attacking such a cooperative ally. Even if he had been able to defeat the Red Army in western Russia, the war was far from over. For Hitler's armies would have been sucked ever farther eastward, while England, aided by America, would continue to pound him from the air. The two-front war he had created would continue. And why take the risk?

Why not remain at peace with his ally and coconspirator and consolidate the vast empire he had gained through his own conquests and the secret protocols of the Nazi-Soviet Pact? He already held in thrall an area stretching from the English Channel to central Poland, from the Baltic to the Mediterranean. Why in the world did he attack the USSR? I tried to respond to such questions in my book.

"WAR WITH THE UNITED STATES WAS ILLOGICAL"

Another problem I confronted was how to explain Hitler's declaration of war on the United States. He had been delighted when Japan attacked Pearl Harbor on 7 December 1941, for that caused America's immediate involvement in war in the Far East. All the Führer needed to do now was to keep his mouth shut and rejoice in his great good fortune.

Instead, four days after Pearl Harbor, he suddenly declared war on the United States, thereby guaranteeing that America's industrial and military power would now be directed against him. That decision, made without consulting either the army or the foreign office, puzzled everybody at the time and historians ever since, for with it he lost irrevocably all hope of winning his war against the Soviet Union. This decision has been called "irrational" and "mysterious."

Since historians are uncomfortable with mysteries — unless they are whodunits — several explanations have been offered. Let's look at two popular ones. It is said that Hitler declared war out of loyalty to his Japanese ally and the fulfillment of his treaty obligation in the Tripartite Pact of 1940 (Germany, Italy, and Japan). But Hitler's sense of honor was not one of his more conspicuous virtues. Moreover, under the pact there was *no obligation whatever* for Germany to support Japan unless the United States attacked Japan. That is not what happened at Pearl Harbor.

It has also been suggested that Hitler decided on war with the United States in early December 1941 because he believed sooner or later the U.S. would attack him, and he wanted to fight at the most advantageous time. It is true that he was always suspicious of President Roosevelt, "that half-Jew who is resolved to go to war and annihilate National Socialism." But the timing of Hitler's decision made no sense.

During the previous week the Red Army, under Marshal Georgi Zhukov, had begun a gigantic counteroffensive using one hundred fresh divisions that Hitler had insisted did not exist. The Germans were hurled back in confusion with enormous losses of men and material. Near panic gripped Hitler's headquarters.

Then, during the first fortnight of December, a blizzard swept the eastern front and again proved, as in the days of Napoleon's ill-fated Grand Army, that Russia's most dreaded field commander was General Winter. Temperatures dropped to minus 30 degrees Fahrenheit, paralyzing the inadequately clothed troops and making transport impossible and weapons unusable. In short, it was the worst possible time for the Führer to add to his troubles by declaring war on the greatest industrial power on earth.

Hitler's declaration of war was a political godsend to President Roosevelt. At one stroke the ground was cut from under FDR's political opponents. For now even the most dedicated noninterventionist in Congress could not object to directing U.S. military efforts against Hitler.

The way Hitler had helped Roosevelt was shown clearly on the very day Hitler declared war. On 11 December, when the President asked Congress for a declaration of war against Germany, not one member of Congress voted against a resolution that, had it been taken only a day earlier, would have been defeated.

Judged in either military or political terms, Hitler's decision to declare war on the United States was an unnecessary and stupid act that benefited his enemies far more than it helped him. The Führer himself admitted in 1944 that it made no sense: "War with the United States was tragic and illogical." He was right about that.

I suppose it is possible that the United States might have been drawn into a shooting war with Hitler at some future time. We can never know. But we do know that Hitler had not only blundered, he had paved the way for his own destruction.

"Our Greatest Enemy Is the Jew, the Eternal Jew"

The most disastrous political decision Hitler made was the result of his lifelong obsession with the "Jewish Peril." Two statements, one at the start of his political career and one at the end, show the persistence of this obsession.

In a document dated September 1919, he stated that his final goal was the "total elimination *(Ausmerzung)* of Jews from Europe." At the end of his career, in April 1945, when he dictated his political testament to the German people, the last word of the last sentence of this last order should be noted: "Above everything else, I charge the leaders of this nation . . . to scrupulous maintenance of racial laws and to merciless attacks on the universal poisoner of all nations, international Jewry."

A fragment of a conversation of 1922, found preserved in a Munich archive, reveals the depth and intensity of Hitler's loathing of the Jewish people, his confidence that he would come to power, and his assurance that when he did, he would do "the work of the Lord" by killing every single Jew in the Fatherland. The method of murder also reveals Hitler's personal preoccupation with filth, stench, putrefaction, and strangulation:

> As soon as I have the power, I shall have gallows after gallows erected, for example in Munich in the Marienplatz . . . Then the Jews will be hanged one after another and they will stay hanging until they stink. They will stay hanging as long as hygienically possible. As soon as they are untied, then the next group will follow. And that will continue until the last Jew in Munich is exterminated.

Exactly the same procedure will be followed in other cities until Germany is cleansed of the last Jew!

Twenty years later, when he did come to power, Hitler would find more efficient methods of mass murder.

In his nightly soliloquies Hitler occasionally mused about resettling Jews in Russia or in Madagascar, but there was one overriding biological reason why resettlement could not finally solve the "Jewish Problem": Hitler had decided that Jewishness was a contagious disease that, if not totally eradicated, would infect and ultimately destroy the German people. "Don't be misled into thinking," he had warned in a speech of 1920, "that you can fight diseases without killing the carrier." In dozens of subsequent speeches he used similar metaphors in repeating the same refrain that Jews are "the poisoners of mankind . . . an evil virus . . . a plague-carrying vermin . . ." and, most often, "a bacillus." These words were not mere figures of speech: "I am the Robert Koch of politics. I discovered that Jews are the bacillus and the ferment of social decomposition."

In the same conversation in which he had suggested "all the Jews should be sent packing to Russia," he stopped himself and added, "but it is no way enough (*keinesweg genug*) to drive them out of Germany. We cannot allow them to return . . . I see no other way than extermination."

Two things are remarkable about his use of this word: first, the sheer number of times he spoke of "extermination" and "annihilation" (*Ausrottung* and *Vernichtung*) and second, his fear that he might not be taken seriously when he used the words. Thus, on 30 January 1942, he reminded his audience that when he had prophesied that the Jews would be annihilated, "people *laughed* at my prophecies." Eight months later, being *laughed* at was still on his mind: "People always *laughed* at me as a prophet. Of those who *laughed* then, in innumerable numbers [sic] no longer *laugh* today, and those who still *laugh* now will perhaps no longer *laugh* a short time from now." Hitler wanted his promise to kill all the Jews of Europe to be taken seriously.

So-called "Hitler revisionists" have tried to argue that Hitler himself was not responsible for the Holocaust; they put the blame on Himmler,

Heydrich, and Eichmann. It is they who are the ones, David Irving tells us, "who pulled the wool over Hitler's eyes." Irving also wants us to believe that Hitler did not know what was happening in the death camps. Both assertions are flat-out wrong.

In Hitler's Germany no one but the Führer could possibly have given the orders for genocide, and Hitler knew from the beginning what was happening to the Jews. This is the conclusion of people who were in a position to know. In an interview after the war, Albert Speer said, "It is not possible that he remained uninformed. He gave the order; that is completely certain." Christa Schroeder, a private secretary who talked daily with the Führer and typed his speeches, memos, and letters, said in an interview, "I can say with certainty that Hitler was informed in complete detail of what was happening . . . He knew about it from the start."

When we ask the simple, sensible question, why in the world did Hitler do it? we can find no sensible answer, for a very good reason: the Holocaust made no political, economic, or cultural sense. The Jews for centuries had been loyal and productive citizens who formed no political threat whatever to the German government. Moreover, they had made enormous contributions in German medicine, art, music, and literature. A disproportionate number had volunteered for service during the Great War.

The Holocaust made no military sense. Indeed, Hitler's obsession with the "Jewish Peril" contributed significantly to Germany's military defeat. As Albert Speer reported, a key reason why Germany never developed an atomic bomb was because Hitler considered physics to be Jewish. Consequently, students in German universities were obliged to study physics without the benefit of Einstein.

Hitler's orders to kill the Jews of occupied Europe resulted in serious disruptions of the national war effort. The sheer logistics of collecting, transporting, killing, and disposing of six million "units" — as Eichmann called human beings — were immense. The project required hundreds of thousands of man-hours devoted entirely to its fulfillment. And the project required other sacrifices. At a time when Germany desperately needed laborers, the Nazi government shipped Jews off to death camps in hundreds of boxcars needed for hauling war supplies. Viewed pragmatically, genocide was counterproductive. During the militarily disastrous years of 1942–1945, Germany simply could not afford to embark on the "Final Solution" to a problem that never existed. It made no sense. But Hitler did not see it that way. His sense of priorities in a national crisis was as clear as it was horrendous: *Nothing mattered so much as killing Jews.*

The pathological fears and rages of one man sent millions of innocent people to their deaths and decided the fate of a nation. Like Hitler's decisions to invade Russia and to declare war on the United States, his launching of the Holocaust was a massive mistake that contributed significantly to his defeat.

KAISER AND FÜHRER
IN TWO WORLD WARS

Wilhelm II and Adolf Hitler bear heavy responsibility for unleashing the two world wars of the twentieth century, but there is a difference in the degree of personal responsibility between the two rulers.

"Before God and history, my conscience is clear. I did not want this war."
— Wilhelm II, 1915

Long before the fateful decision in July 1914 that launched the Great War, Wilhelm had demonstrated a remarkable proclivity for alarming other countries, tossing matches into inflammatory material, and pouring petrol onto the ensuing fires. In an age of supercharged nationalism he delivered flamboyantly chauvinistic speeches that threatened peace, and he refused to contemplate any restrictions on the arms race. When the World Court at the Hague sought to arbitrate international disputes and set limits on the excesses of war, the Kaiser announced that he would defecate on their resolutions.

The Kaiser liked to remind everybody that he and no one else was the "Captain of the German Ship." He personally selected the crew and he charted the course that led — in his words "full speed ahead" — into the cataclysm. He could have given orders to sail in a different direction.

Most crucially, the Kaiser could have chosen not to give Austria the "blank check" of unrestricted support. Without Wilhelm's personal, flat assurance that he would support Austria in *any action whatever it might take against Serbia,* Austria would not have started a war in the Balkans that everyone knew could not be localized.

The German general staff had long planned a two-front war against France and Russia. Wilhelm II may have been correct when he spent the rest of his life insisting that he did not want the war. But his generals did, and he did nothing to dissuade them.

The German constitution states that the decision for making war rests *solely* with the Kaiser. Every document authorizing the opening of hostilities bears one unmistakable signature: "Wilhelm II, I.R." These indispensable signatures, with their grand flourishes, were not acts of bold leadership; they were symbols of acquiescence. In the last analysis, the First World War started because Wilhelm II lacked the will and the courage to oppose the war plans of his Great General Staff.

"THE RESOLVE TO STRIKE
WAS ALWAYS WITHIN ME"

The Kaiser's personal responsibility for World War I has been debated
in thousands of scholarly pages. There is no such debate about the
Führer's responsibility for World War II. From the moment he came to
power in 1933 he planned and lusted for war.

He had looked forward to war in 1938 during the Czech crisis
and felt thwarted by Neville Chamberlain's Munich Accord. "No son
of a bitch *(Schweinhund),*" he snarled, was going to deprive him of
war next time. Chamberlain promised that his meeting with Hitler
would bring "peace in our time," but during that calendar year, Hitler
spent more on weapons of war than Britain, France, and the United
States *combined.*

The Kaiser was pushed into war by his generals. No one pushed the
Führer. War came because he wanted it; as he said, war was "always
within me" — in his guts, his sinews, and his psyche.

The two rulers reacted very differently after signing the documents
that launched both wars.

Wilhelm was appalled by what he had done. Distraught and sleep-
less, he spent anxious hours seeking solace in prayer. He was found in
tears praying for hours in corners of churches all over the Rhineland.
On 31 August 1939, after signing Order No. 1 that would send the
Wehrmacht crashing into Poland the next morning, Hitler was in a state
of euphoria all day, and then he had a very good night's sleep.

As military leaders, there was a vast difference in the performances of
Kaiser and Führer.

Wilhelm had always seen himself as a heroic military commander. He liked to dress in any one of more than 250 uniforms; he supervised the painting of his portrait as Mars, the apotheosis of war; he gloried in his official titles, Supreme War Lord and The All-Highest Person *(Die allerhöchste Person)*. But when the war came in 1914, he abjectly surrendered his power to the generals. His high-flying titles became hollow mockeries. He himself petulantly described the position he had put himself in: "The General Staff tells me nothing and never asks my advice. If anyone in Germany imagines that I lead the army, they are badly mistaken . . . I drink tea, saw wood and go for walks. And then I learn from time to time that this or that has been done, just as the *Herren* [of the General Staff] wanted."

In the first war, the Kaiser constantly acquiesed to the generals. In the second war, the Führer steadily increased his power as supreme commander of all Germany's armed forces. After his smashing victories in France, the Low Countries, and Norway, the Führer came to despise his generals who had doubted his military genius. When some of them plotted against him in July 1944, he had them hanged on meat hooks, strangled by slowly tightening piano wire. He liked to watch, over and over, the slow-motion, colored movies of their agonizing deaths.

PSYCHOLOGICAL DIMENSIONS

In thinking about the careers of Kaiser and Führer in peace and in war, I kept puzzling over the question of why both rulers of keen intelligence often acted irrationally. Why did Wilhelm keep saying and doing things that were bound to alienate the very people who could help him? Why did he keep defeating his own purposes? Why was his conduct in both domestic and foreign affairs so erratic? Why did Hitler hate the Jews with such incandescent intensity? Why was he compelled to take unnecessary gambles and persistently court disaster? Since I was unable to answer those questions and became convinced that I was dealing with two pathological personalities, I sought the help of psychopathologists.

I was warned against doing so. A respected English historian, for instance, told me that he totally disagreed with my approach. He said that throughout his long career he had relied on his "greatest gift, plain, good old-fashioned common sense." And who would dispute the manifold blessings of common sense?

The problem is that it is not much help in dealing with historical personalities who refuse to act sensibly. Hitler, for instance, launched the Holocaust and that event made no sense on any grounds, cultural, economic, political, or military. The question remains: Why did he do it? To conclude simply that his actions are "inexplicable " or that he was "deranged" does very little to further our understanding.

On the other hand, "psychohistorians" sometimes become so enamored of their approach and so intrigued by the psychologically rich data provided for them by Kaiser and Führer that they ignore more prosaic types of evidence and write as if all aspects of their subjects' careers can be reduced to psychopathological analysis. I disagree and reached the conclusion that psychology can be *helpful;* no greater — and no lesser — claim than that should be made. As St. Thomas Aquinas said about the power of reason, psychological understanding is "essential but not sufficient."

I found that the mental condition called "narcissistic personality" offered me the best clues to understanding the Kaiser's behavior; I found that the Führer's pathology is best seen as "borderline personality disorder." But my purpose was to increase my understanding, not to reduce complex personalities to neat textbook labels. I was particularly interested in seeing the ways in which the personal pathologies of both rulers affected their public policies. I found that the peculiar personalities of both Kaiser and Führer were a considerable asset to them: Both were in tune with their times.

The cocky, narcissistic flamboyance of the young Kaiser harmonized with the confident exuberance of the newly united country. The new ruler and the new nation were both impatiently ambitious. In asserting his grandiosity and power, Wilhelm was driven by his own psychic need to deny feelings of inadequacy and to force others to respect him. These personal needs were shared by Germans who also longed to be accepted and respected. An editorial of 1913, the silver jubilee of his reign, summed up the symbiotic relationship between Wilhelm and his people: "Our Kaiser expresses the spirit of the new era, and the era is the expression of the spirit of our Kaiser."

But problems of personality also posed problems for his policy. Lacking cohesion within himself, Wilhelm was never able to develop a coherent policy in either domestic or foreign affairs. Moreover, his narcissistic distrust of others would not permit him to let anyone else set a coherent policy.

The disastrous effect on foreign policy of his personal suspiciousness was manifest on the eve of war. Wilhelm could not make peace in 1914 because there was no one he could trust. The English foreign secretary was a "deceitful scoundrel"; the French were "lying hypocrites"; Nicholas

II of Russia's peace efforts were so many "sly maneuvers." The world of Wilhelm's pathological imagining was one in which serious negotiation was impossible.

Adolf Hitler's personality was also in harmony with the Germany of his times. A proud people who had been humiliated by military defeat and betrayed by "the treaty of shame" were consumed by feelings of hatred, and they hungered for revenge. So did Hitler. Germans found him, as one man told me, "one of us" — a leader who, like them, had also known humiliation, defeat, and abuse. He renewed their sense of pride and power and gave them a chance to mobilize their hatred. This hate-filled man spoke their language. "I demand of you," he yelled in a speech of 10 April 1923, "pride, willpower, defiance, and hatred, and again, hatred!" The crowd roared approval.

Hitler became one of the most compelling demagogues in history because his personal resentments coincided with the resentments of the German people. Without their approval he could never have established one of the most vicious and certainly the most popular tyranny the world has ever known.

Hitler's grandiose fantasies were also a political asset. Realists have said that his appeal was largely an appeal merely to myths and illusions — the illusion of Jewish menace, the myth of a "pure-souled Aryan race," the illusion of an infallible Führer. The realists were correct, but they failed to appreciate the power of illusion in human affairs. Hitler knew how desperately the German people, after the defeat of their unde-featable army in the Great War and their own failure with democracy, wanted to believe in heroic myths. By the alchemy of Hitler's charisma and the force of his propaganda, the cherished myths of German history were Nazified and made irresistible to millions of citizens. To them Hitler became the long-awaited Barbarossa, the Germanic hero who would create a new and mightier Reich of the German nation.

Hitler's mythmaking also served an important personal function. His illusion that he was the infallible Man of Destiny saved him from complete psychological disintegration in 1945 when he was confronted by physical deterioration and the collapse of all his personal dreams.

Through all his defeats, he retained his unshakable conviction that he would yet prevail. This grandiose self-image was also a political asset, for he conveyed his illusions to the German people. They, too, were convinced that the Führer could not fail.

But belief in his infallibility also produced rigid, obdurate consistency — a hallmark of the borderline personality — that proved a liability. At Stalingrad and the final battle for Berlin, the Führer's obstinacy meant military disaster and the needless sacrifice of hundreds of thousands of young German lives. When told how many young men were dying, he replied characteristically: "Well, what are young people for?"

Doubts about his own masculinity continually drove him to prove his omnipotence. Hitler was condemned to stay on the offense. To go on the defensive or to negotiate was to confess a feminine weakness. When it was suggested very late in the war that Germany ought to sue for peace, Hitler flew into a frenzy: "Never will I capitulate . . . that word means surrender as a woman surrenders to a man. *Kapitulation?* Never! I do not know that word and I will never know . . . it is the surrender of the will to another person. *Never! Never! Never!"*

And so it continued to the end. Because Adolf Hitler personally could not surrender, the country had to perish. It was less painful for him to see Germany destroyed than for him to capitulate.

LIMITATIONS OF PSYCHOLOGY

I found the counsel of psychotherapists and the literature they suggested immensely helpful in my efforts to understand the baffling behavior of both Kaiser and Führer. In my view, however, there are dimensions of human experience that do not yield to psychological analysis.

Psychology, to take one example, helped me understand how Wilhelm's narcissistic self-glorification and the fantasy that Hitler would soon restore him to power enabled him to weather the shocks of humiliation, defeat, and exile. Yet the ex-Kaiser himself said that, above everything else, it was daily prayer and his deep Christian faith that sustained him. And personal religious faith, as Anthony Burgess remarked, can no more yield to psychoanalysis than music can yield to mathematics.

Similarly, psychological studies of borderline personalities gave me a deeper understanding of Adolf Hitler's strange behavior; but, again, the therapists I consulted could not explain the *intensity* of Hitler's hatred. Certainly, "psychic injury" had been done to him — as it has been done to millions of other human beings — but what was it that drove Hitler to commit such unspeakable evil? I cannot answer that question, but I must recognize that his consuming hatred was a driving force behind his atrocities.

Nor can psychological analysis fully account for another quality that I found to characterize this extraordinary man: his internal strength — the tough, resilient fiber that set Hitler apart from hundreds of other pathological personalities. It enabled him to overcome moments of self-doubt and to retain until the very end his unshakable confidence in himself and his destiny. This quality may, in the end, come down to a simple act of will. And that, too, is a dimension of the man that resists psychological analysis. But, again, my inability to explain it does not reduce its importance.

Nor was psychology able to help me solve what has been called the "ultimate mystery" of Hitler: the overwhelming personal magnetism of the man. One of his generals reported that when he was in the presence of his Führer, "I was drained of any will of my own." Albert Speer, who was determined to oppose Hitler, melted in his presence and blurted out, "My Führer, I stand unconditionally behind you." And how in the world can we explain the incredible attraction women had to this peculiar little man?

Finally, psychotherapists were not able to help me in understanding a key question regarding the essential difference between Kaiser and Führer. I found striking similarities between the two men, but ultimately the difference was this: Adolf Hitler was evil, Wilhelm von Hohenzollern was not. He was capricious, foolish, sometimes mean-spirited, and even cruel, but he was not an evil person.

That word "evil" poses big problems for psychotherapists. They take professional pride in remaining dispassionate and "value free." As one of them told me, "Sure, I might agree with you personally, but as a professional psychotherapist I am not in the business of making moral judgments." I could not find the word "evil" listed in the index of any standard psychiatric lexicon.

Yet evil is a part of the human psyche. It is present in the Unabomber and in the late Pol Pot, and in anyone who rapes a four-year-old girl. It was manifested in the perpetrators of Auschwitz and My Lai, and in the racial cleansers of Kosovo. It was at the core of Hitler's being. How can such evil be explained?

It is not given to us humans to understand one another completely. Ultimately, we remain a mystery. Perhaps that's just as well.

L'ENVOI:
"Where Do You Keep Your Mops?"

The final stages of my personal academic procession started one melancholy autumnal day in 1988 when I was asked, ever so politely, to clear out of my office. For most of my forty years at Williams I had occupied a spacious room on the top floor of Stetson Hall, then the college library, looking out onto the Green Mountains of Vermont. It was a fine office where I had spent many memorable hours.

Here I had wrestled with the black despair and subdued suicidal impulses during that first awful month at the college; here I had prayed for strength and peace; here I had felt the exhilaration of a successful class or a lecture that had gone well — as well as gloom when a class session had gone badly; here I had counseled lonely freshmen and guided the research of senior honors theses; here I had written much of my first book; here I had brought my three-year-old son, who looked out the window at the Vermont hills and said, "Daddy, this is the tallest I've ever been."

Of course I had known for some time that I would be obliged to give it up when I retired, and that it would go to a younger man. That was completely understandable and to be expected. I would share with an older colleague a small "emeriti office" in the basement, adjacent to the offices of new instructors. We could work out a schedule of hours during which each of us would use the room.

As I began moving my books, notes, and other chattel out of their familiar surroundings, I was afflicted with the "has-been syndrome" and a wave of an all-too-familiar depression. A new instructor's question did nothing to lift my spirits.

227

"Hey, where do you keep your mops?"

I was wearing an old work shirt and moving things around on the basement floor, when he came up to me and asked, "Hey, where do you keep your mops?" I told him. They were right next door.

The following Saturday morning, the college staged its opening fall convocation with a formal academic procession. As a new emeritus, I marched in my crimson gown toward the head of the parade. As the procession reversed direction, the end of the line came alongside the front, and I found myself looking directly into the face of my mop quester. He looked aghast when he saw me. For days he tried to avoid meeting me in the basement, until I invited him for a cup of coffee and we laughed together about the mops.

Academics have at least one advantage not shared by salesmen and surgeons: Our professional careers need not terminate when we retire. When we no longer teach, we can continue our research and writing.

I moved a word processor into my shared office and began writing my Kaiser-Hitler book, which I continued when, in 1989, I was asked by the college president, Francis Oakley, to be a Senior Fellow of the recently opened Williams Center for Humanities and Social Sciences — soon to be renamed the Francis Christopher Oakley Center. We are indebted to Ocean Spray Cranberries for funding the center.

Charles Makepeace, an alumnus of the college, had inherited Ocean Spray Cranberries Inc. from his father, who had been known as "King Cranberry" for popularizing the humble berry and making it indispensable for turkey dinners. Makepeace, who became the Treasurer of Williams College — indeed, had signed my appointment letter in 1949 with its stipulation of a munificent salary of $4,000 — had built a spacious home near the college campus. After his widow's death, the house was willed, along with a generous financial settlement, to the college.

President Oakley noted that the natural sciences had been handsomely endowed by the Bronfman family — I'll talk about that in a minute — and decided to use the Makepeace bequest for the humanities and social studies. Every year some eight Fellows are appointed from the faculty: two Seniors and six regular Fellows. Each is given a private office, secretarial assistance, and an annual stipend. Fellows have no teaching obligations; their sole responsibility is to their own research and professional development. Once a week Fellows meet for a bag lunch and report to their colleagues on their research in progress. Fellowships are particularly welcomed by junior members of the faculty who want to complete their doctoral dissertation or get out a first book.

I profited from my two-year stint as a Senior Fellow, for, in addition to giving me time to write a good part of the Kaiser-Hitler book, the center financed my research trip to Doorn House and the National Dutch Archives in Utrecht.

Frank Oakley had come to the Williams history department from teaching at Yale. I remember reviewing his dossier when he was being "looked over" here. One of his mentors at Corpus Christi College, Oxford, Oakley's undergraduate college, spoke highly of his academic achievement. Then, to suggest he had more arrows in his quiver, the mentor noted his role in an undergraduate drama society and concluded, with marvelous British ambivalence, "He also did some *rather useful cross-country running*" — a statement that could mean either that he was an Olympic medal winner or that he occasionally ran for his college. I have the vision of Frank Oakley running "usefully" past the seventeenth hole of the Taconic golf course here in town. While teaching at Williams he continued his distinguished publications in Medieval history.

Prior to the presidency of Francis Oakley (1985–1993), I had served under three other able leaders who had also facilitated and enriched my academic procession.

James Phinney Baxter III (1937–1961) was an extraordinarily gifted and complex man. A noted American diplomatic historian and Master of Adams House at Harvard before he returned to his alma mater as president, he had written a standard work on the development of iron-clad warships. During the Second World War, he took a leave of absence from Williams to serve as Deputy Director of the OSS and historian in the Office of Scientific Research and Development. His experience in the latter office enabled him to write a Pulitzer Prize-winning study of the contributions American scientists had made to the war effort: *Scientists Against Time.*

Baxter had a volcanic temper and sometimes displayed the manners of a warthog. Yet he could be kind and gentle as well as courageous in defending academic freedom. When his board of trustees wanted to fire political science professor Frederick Schuman for not being sufficiently anti-Communist, Phinney, who was himself a staunch Republican, told the board, "The day you ask for his resignation, gentlemen, you will have mine." During the McCarthy period he stood solidly behind all his faculty.

Personally, I shall always be in his debt, for without his humane intervention it is probable that my academic career would have collapsed at the very outset. I had been teaching at Williams for only a couple of months when, just before Thanksgiving 1949, I went into a mental tailspin and suffered the terrifying experience of total depression. Drained of all confidence, terrified by the thought of facing a class, I went to the chairman of the history department and told him I was a total failure, that he never should have hired me, and that I ought to be fired. He went to President Baxter and recommended that my contract be canceled immediately. Baxter flatly rejected his proposal.

Sensing my distress, Mr. Baxter asked Anne to come to his office. The first thing he told her was that he had complete confidence in me, that he himself had once been on the ropes and he understood my problem. He asked her to tell me that I was certainly not going to be fired, that I needed help, he would see that I got it, and I was to take a paid leave of absence until I felt better. My job would be waiting for me. He also personally arranged for me to see a psychiatrist he knew in Minneapolis, Anne's home.

The sensible doctor did not attempt any "depth analysis." The most helpful thing he did was to ask me the location of Williams College — he had never heard of the place! That amazed me, for I had been convinced that it was the center of the academic universe. His simple question helped me see my problems in perspective.

Briefly, I pulled through the crisis thanks to this man's wise counseling and the grace of God. All my life I have had faith in God and the power of prayer. That faith sustained me now. A great darkness had been lifted and I felt at peace. After Christmas I started the spring term with enthusiasm and renewed confidence.

One of my favorite stories about Phinney Baxter took place during a fall convocation. At this formal affair, Phinney, who was seated center stage, was seen slumping during one of the speeches. He then straightened up momentarily and slumped down again. Concern grew that the old man had suffered a heart attack. Someone discreetly approached him to offer assistance, when he saw that President Baxter was surreptitiously listening to a small transistor radio hidden under his gown, that was carrying the Red Sox playoff game. (Perhaps it is needless to report that the Sox were defeated.)

Baxter's honors student in history and successor, John E. Sawyer, was a superb administrator under whose skillful guidance (1961–1973) four major innovations that greatly improved the college were instituted. I heartily endorsed them all.

First, he ended compulsory chapel. I am a religious person who believes in going to church, but I find the idea of making church attendance "compulsory" deeply repugnant.

Second, he abolished the fraternity system, which had been a blight on the college for many years. Many sentimental alumni with glowing memories of happy fraternal days were outraged and praised the many benefits they thought they had gained from their fraternities. I and many other faculty members saw the matter differently. We had counseled too many heartsick freshmen who had been told at the age of seventeen that they were not good enough to belong. Sawyer, himself a fraternity man, wisely chose a strong committee chaired by a popular and successful ex-fraternity man who submitted an impressive report that so weakened the fraternity system it was subsequently abolished. When the report was accepted, a few disgruntled alumni withdrew their financial support and predicted a dramatic decline in alumni giving. They were mistaken. Alumni giving rose significantly.

Third, Williams became coeducational. Female students have been an important social and academic asset to the college. Women tend to be better students who work harder than their male counterparts. Since males didn't like to be shown up in discussion classes, male performance improved.

Fourth, under Sawyer and his successors the college has significantly expanded its social and racial composition. When I arrived in 1949 Williams was predominantly WASP, with some 64 percent of the student body drawn from preparatory schools of New England. When I left in 1988, that statistic was reversed: 64 percent came from public high schools from across the country and more than 30 percent came from minority racial groups. In short, we now have a student body much more representative of the country and more stimulating to teach.

Also during Sawyer's administration, a large science center financed by the Bronfman family was erected. Samuel Bronfman was the Canadian financier who purchased Seagram and Company and made a fortune selling whiskey to Americans during the Prohibition era. His son and successor, Edgar, later the distinguished president of the World Jewish Congress, had not had a distinguished academic career at Williams. Indeed, he was invited to leave. When faculty members learned that Bronfman senior had been planning a major gift to the college, they predicted that the expulsion of the son would mean the loss of Bronfman largesse. They were mistaken. The old man expressed respect for the college that expelled his son.

Years later, Edgar and the other children of Samuel Bronfman contributed generously to endow the handsome Bronfman Science Center, which was dedicated in 1968.

"Let's Stop This Chickenshit"

Normally, I had not participated in college politics. But the months between March 1969 and April 1970, during John Sawyer's administration, were not normal times.

This was the height of the Vietnam War and the campus was in turmoil. At 8 A.M. on April 1969, the first anniversary of Martin Luther King's death, the Afro-American students took over Hopkins Hall, the administration building on campus. Anne and I were particularly concerned because a black student was living in our home with us. Thanks to the intelligent leadership of both the black leader, Preston Washington, '70, and the college administrator in charge of negotiation, Provost Stephen Lewis, '60, the black students, after three days, left the administration building without damage or sabotage. The "unnegotiable demands" were negotiated.

Six months later, on Vietnam Memorial Day, 15 October 1969, a petition bearing 2,300 signatures (1,262 townspeople and 932 students, 106 faculty members, the president and the trustees of the college) was sent to Washington protesting the war. That day the college chapel was filled for prayer service and pleas for peace. That same day, Chaplain John Eusden and Professor Robert Waite led a peaceful march of some 2,500 students and townspeople, "Pause for Peace," to the Eastlawn cemetery.

The following 5 May 1970, President Nixon stepped up the war and Jack Sawyer wrote an open letter to 14,000 alumni and parents: "I have seen no evidence that this war can achieve any purpose commensurate with its costs."

That day President Nixon, without consulting Congress, also ordered American troops to invade neutral Cambodia. Williams students voted overwhelmingly for a symbolic strike. That evening they overfilled Chapin Hall, the largest auditorium on campus. I quote from the *Williams Record* of 8 May 1970, which bore one word two and one-half inches high on its first page: *STRIKE!*

> *The Williams campus has exploded . . . In the midst of confusion there is purpose, and amid dispersion, an uncharacteristic unity . . .*
>
> *Wednesday night in Chapin Hall, over 1,300 people gathered to hear the announcement of the Faculty's proposal for dealing with the remaining portion of the academic year in light of the indefinite strike . . . The next half-hour was spent in insignificant questions and petty complaints about the proposal.*
>
> *At last, history Prof. Robert G. L. Waite stood up and cut through the administrative question with energy, emotion and clear thinking, as he said, "Let's stop this chickenshit and get on with the issue." The onlookers again broke into wild applause and gave Mr. Waite a standing ovation.*

I had never thought I would ever curse in front of the entire Williams undergraduate body, and I wondered what the repercussions would be. The next day I was called into President Sawyer's office. He laughed and thanked me for my "eloquent speech."

"Williams in Oxford"

While John Wesley Chandler was president (1973–1985), he had the imagination and foresight to purchase in Oxford an enclave of buildings forming a small quad, which became the "Williams in Oxford" program. Each year about thirty undergraduates attend from Williams and five from Oxford's Exeter College. Williams students take their tutorials from Exeter dons as well as instructors from other Oxford colleges. They also participate in college dramatics, tennis, and rowing. Over the years Williams students have held their own in a program that has been a resounding success.

Williams in Oxford was a great boon to me personally, for it maintained a spacious and completely furnished apartment that visiting Williams faculty could use for a fortnight, a term, or a year. Anne and I enjoyed using the facility on five happy occasions during which I continued my research on the Kaiser.

ANNE'S ILLNESS AND DEATH

I continued writing the Kaiser-Hitler book at Sweetwood, Williamstown, a retirement community set in the Berkshire Hills. Anne and I had planned to move into our flat together, but she was hit by a major stroke in 1991 that affected the frontal lobe of her brain and left her paralyzed. She was moved to a private room in a nursing home within walking distance of Sweetwood, where I could visit her daily.

Her whole personality had changed. She was able to speak only a few words and had no capacity for empathy, warmth, or humor. For months she suffered the anguish of knowing something was terribly wrong but not knowing what it was. When Geoffrey and Peter came to visit her, she recognized them as her sons, but they evoked no more apparent emotional reaction than a janitor or a mailman. When I told her that Peter had dedicated his first one-man show in New York "To My Mother," she said in a flat voice, "That's nice."

I reminded Anne of walks we had enjoyed together: around Lake Harriet in Minneapolis when I went a-courtin' from Fort Snelling; along the Charles River in Cambridge and the River Walk in San Antonio; through the main street of Fredericksburg, Texas, and stopping to buy the Lola Montez brooch; walking along the banks of the Isis and the Charwell in Oxford; along the Neva in Leningrad; through the English Gardens in Munich; along the Great Wall in China and the long path leading out of King Tut's tomb in Egypt.

I also recited psalms and poems. The night she lay dying, I reminded her of the night we had fallen in love on a blind date and had recited verse to each other; how I had got stuck on *Young Lochinvar* and she had helped me out. She said, "Say it now." So I did: "Oh, young Lochinvar is come out of the West, / Through all the wide border his steed was the best . . ." Anne seemed to be sinking fast; I prayed and then recited the poem she had taught me on our blind date:

Into my heart's treasury I slipped a coin
Which time cannot take or a thief purloin.
Oh, better than the minting of a gold-crowned king
Is the safe-kept memory of a lovely thing.

She smiled, squeezed my hand, and died.

I walked home through a light snow on a cold winter night, weeping and laughing and thanking God for the years we had had together.

Anne's memorial service well filled the First Congregational Church. Geoffrey came from Ithaca, where he is professor of Germanic studies, Peter from Hartford, where he is a successful artist. The pastor and the college chaplain both paid thoughtful, lighthearted tributes to Anne that she would have appreciated. I wore the bow tie she had given me for Christmas in Felton Hall and spoke briefly about our happy years together. The congregation sang our family hymn, "Now Thank We All Our God," and Anne's favorite, the lovely Irish hymn dating from the eighth century:

Be Thou my vision, O Lord of my heart;
Naught be all else to me save that Thou art.
Thou my best thought, by day or by night,
Waking or sleeping, Thy presence my light.

During the months after Anne's death, I was grateful to the Kaiser and the Führer for giving me something to occupy my time. I finished writing the book. But I could not have done it without the support and encouragement of my friend and former colleague, Fred H. Stocking, the Morris

Professor of Rhetoric, Emeritus. His keen editorial eye helped me organize a complex manuscript. His sense of style was indispensable. With exemplary patience and good humor he labored mightily over several drafts to discipline and smooth out my sometimes excessive and uneven prose.

After several American publishers were put off by the book's length and extensive documentation and their suspicion that the Kaiser would not sell well in the United States, I was delighted when it was accepted by the University of Toronto Press, whose editors have been knowledgeable, considerate, and altogether a pleasure to work with.

• • • • •

In looking back over my own academic procession, most of it spent at Williams College, it strikes me that the college has been blessed by its magnificent location, by the excellence of its presidential leadership, and by the quality of its faculty, students, and alumni.

The college enjoys remarkable support from its graduates. Each year more than 60 percent of its alumni give to the Alumni Fund — an unusually high percentage among the college alumni associations of America. The Williams Alumni Association — which is the oldest in the world — has been remarkably creative.

Under the able and imaginative direction of Robert V. Behr of the Alumni Office, a program of continuing education for alumni has been particularly successful. Professors are invited to lecture during alumni cruises on trips to destinations all over the world: from Greenland to Antarctica, from the Galapagos to the capitals of the Baltic, and to Australia, India, and China, from Istanbul up the Danube and the Rhine to Cologne; on the art and architecture of France, of Germany, and of England. In preparing lectures for several of these excursions, I have discovered that the "continuing education" applies not only to former students of Williams but also to their professors.

For instance, in giving six lectures on "makers of Germany" for an alumni trip on the Rhine, I was obliged to do a great deal of new research on Charlemagne, the giant who bestrode the Continent and established the "First Reich of the German Nation." I also learned more about Hildegard of Bingen (1198–1290), one of the most fascinating women of history, about whom I had known little before this cruise. She was abbess, poet, musician, biologist, artist, biographer, religious mystic, and sexologist. Kings and popes sought her counsel; she was exorciser of demons and scourge of corrupt clergy; she preached in Trier and in Cologne. Her tongue is preserved in a reliquary in the parish church of Rödesheim, a town we would visit on the banks of the Rhine.

In lecturing on India in the fall of 1999, I shall want to talk about Hinduism, at once the most inclusive and absorptive of the world's great religions. I will also discuss important leaders such as the Buddha; the Moguls, Babur, and Akbar the Great, and — because her husband can be forgotten — that remarkable Mogul empress, Nur Jahan (1611–1645), who designed textiles, built lovely gardens, wrote Persian poetry and composed music, designed and supervised the erection of three tombs, was counselor of an Islamic state and worshiper of the Virgin Mary. I shall also need to speak of the British Raj and the rise of independence, Gandhi and Nehru and the resulting republic.

Education never stops.

The association has also sponsored alumni seminars held each year during class reunion weekends. It also invites faculty members to talk about their professional interests to any of seventy-nine alumni associations throughout the country, from Dallas to Seattle, from Boston and Minneapolis-St. Paul to San Francisco and Honolulu. I have found these audiences among the most critical and stimulating of my experience. It's good to know that former students remain hungry for substantive intellectual fare.

I particularly enjoyed one such experience. In March 1974 I had been invited to speak to the Williams Alumni Association of Chicago. Anne and I were put up in an enormous guest suite in the Drake Hotel on the Gold Coast. When I remarked to the president of the association that I had come to help raise a little money rather than to spend it so lavishly, he told me not to worry, the owner of the hotel was an alumnus.

We had two king-size beds, two dressing rooms, two bathrooms, and a conference room. All very impressive, but in the middle of the night — as is my custom — I found myself trying urgently to find a facility. After scurrying sleepily through several rooms, I finally found what I was looking for, but not quite in time.

When we had arrived, I noted that one of the beds had not been made up. I rang the housekeeper and asked about changing the sheets. She appeared before me to ask if I really wanted them changed: "I think you should know that Doris Day slept in those very sheets last night!" I said bully for her, but I'd like fresh ones.

Peter Waite, who had started his career as an artist on the Thomamüllers' kitchen table in Ottobrunn, was to get his MFA at the School of the Art Institute of Chicago that June. I knew we would not be able to fly out for his graduation, so suggested that we celebrate the occasion while his mother and I were in town. I invited him and four or five of his friends to join us in our suite for wine and cheese before going out for dinner at an inexpensive spaghetti joint he knew.

As we were sitting around the large cocktail table in the conference room, one of the art students suggested we play The Game — which consisted of asking questions that could be answered with the name of a well-known artist. For instance, "What artist reminds you of a festive occasion?" Answer: "'Tis the Cezanne to be jolly"; or "What is the answer to the question 'Kandinsky?'" Answer: "Maybe not, but he's a helluva hockey player."

When my turn arrived, I saw Peter anxiously giving me a Dad-don't-let-me-down-now look. The pressure mounted.

Probably because I was in what my dad would have called "parlous straits," memories of my father flashed through my mind: his great sense of fun, how he would have enjoyed the "five coffees and one beer" story and how he — the master of atrocious puns — would have mastered the game we were playing.

Suddenly, I had a bright idea — as in comic strips when a light bulb flashes over the head of someone badly in need of an idea. This time the light was turned on, I like to think, by my punning father intervening from the Great Beyond to rescue his apprehensive son. He who had inspired me so often in the past inspired me now. I asked, "What's the worst thing that can happen to a Canadian trapper in northern Quebec?" When no one responded, I said, "Toulouse-Lautrec."

• • • • •

Well, it's been a long trip from Franklin and Swan River to Winnipeg, from Benson High School to Harvard and Oxford and Voorhees College, from Portal to Temagami and Williamstown. And I have hugely enjoyed it.

With the exception of that week taking care of John Wilkes Booth, I have been handsomely paid for what I would have loved to do gratis: read history, the subject I love, and talk and write about it. As I look back on my academic career, I am filled with gratitude and I think of the psalmist: "The lines have fallen for me in pleasant places; yea, I have a good inheritance . . . Praise the Lord, O my soul!"

I am grateful for the opportunity given me of teaching under-graduates — although I never found it relaxing. If a class went well, I was exhilarated; if it went badly, I was depressed. It was intellectually challenging to present historical events and people in such a way that they came alive to students, but to do so in ways that did no violence to historical accuracy. Constantly I felt called upon to serve two masters: my students and my commitment to scholarship. When I failed, I would leave the classroom with an uneasy conscience.

I enjoyed doing research and working in the archives in Windsor Castle, Berlin, Vienna, Munich, and Utrecht. My life has been enriched by the vivid and wonderfully helpful people I have encountered in my research: Lord Alexander of Tunis; Hans and Käthe Thomamüller of Ottobrunn; Tony Nicholls of St. Antony's, Oxford; Erik Erikson and Norbert Blomberg; Franz Jetzinger, the Linz archivist; Sir David Frost; Lord Alan Bullock; L. J. Verroen, the curator of Doorn House; Betty Kohut and Eitel Proelss of Sweetwood.

My efforts to combine the insights of history and psychology in seeking a deeper understanding of Wilhelm von Hohenzollern and Adolf

Hitler have widened my appreciation of the complexities of human life.

In the end, historical writing is an act of imaginative reconstruction. My efforts to reconstruct past events and dead personalities must remain fallible, flawed, and incomplete. I am often reminded of Henry James's wise admonition: "Never say you know the last word about the human heart."

FINIS